THE ROAD BACK

— A JOURNEY OF GRACE AND GRIT —

BY MICHAEL VITEZ

Winner of the Pulitzer Prize

B MILLER

ISBN: 1475073089
ISBN 13: 9781475073089
Library of Congress Control Number: 2012906230
CreateSpace, North Charleston, South Carolina

CHAPTER ONE

Mark Harris didn't know what caused the cyclist to spill over the double yellow line, and fall into the path of the oncoming blue Porsche, but he saw it happen. He saw the rider hit the sports car, flip into the air, and land on the asphalt. "That boy's dead," he said to his wife.

Harris doesn't remember slamming on his own brakes, running to the boy's side. But he got there first.

The boy wasn't breathing, and he was making the kind of posturing – arms and legs straight, rigid – that indicated significant brain damage. He was bleeding out of his mouth and from his ear, sure signs of a skull fracture. His face was completely crushed. Mark Harris just happened to be Dr. Mark Harris, an anesthesiologist. The doctor, who was only seconds ago enjoying a peaceful ride with his classic car club, assessed his options and made a "battlefield decision" to move aggressively. "If he has a neck injury he might be paralyzed," Harris thought to himself. "But if I don't do something to get him breathing again, he'll be dead."

Harris cradled the bleeding youth in his lap. His jaw was fractured on both sides and was completely loose. All his teeth were smashed. The cyclist was unconscious, motionless. Harris turned him on his side, so all the blood would spill into the doctor's lap rather than down the boy's throat. He cleared out the broken teeth with his fingers, and then – what almost no one else on the planet and even few doctors would have known to do – he tugged the boy's shattered jaw forward.

"It's a painful stimulus," Harris explained later. "The idea is if you provide a painful stimulus, they will breathe on their own. I hurt him as best I could to get him to breathe."

The boy started to breathe.

Rudy Kahsar and Chris Morrow, members of the University of Virginia triathlon club, had been riding with their classmate, Matt Miller, and reached him about the same instant as Dr. Harris, who told them to dial 911. Rudy had his cell phone, but couldn't get any reception, not even one bar. Right at that section of the Blue Ridge Parkway, milepost 12.2, there is a high steep ridge on one side of the road, and that might have been blocking any cell reception. Rudy saw a collection of giant boulders, and climbed to the top of them, hoping the added elevation might give him better reception. "I've got to get higher," he told himself, and scrambled up as high as he could get, and got one bar on his phone. Maybe that was a miracle, too, just like an anesthesiologist being in the very last car of the classic car caravan, right behind the blue Porsche, and so Rudy called 911 so many times the Augusta County dispatcher asked him to stop calling. Then he ran back to the others, who were with Matt.

Mary Ann Harris took her husband's walkie-talkie and tried to radio ahead, but of course the walkie-talkie didn't work. All the other 30 cars in the caravan just motored on down the road toward the Peaks of Otter Lodge, not a clue what had happened – except for one, a red Austin Healy, third from last in the caravan. The driver must have seen in his rearview mirror what had happened, or at least that something had happened, and he pulled over and ran back to the accident scene. The driver of the red Austin Healy began to tell Mark Harris what to do. "Shouldn't you lay him flat on his back?" The man had no idea who Mark Harris was, other than another member of their car club. But the man seemed to think that whatever Harris was doing was wrong. Mark is a gentle and soft-spoken man. But this was a battlefield situation – as Mark would say, like being on Anzio Beach – and he dispensed with cordiality. "I do this every f– ing day," he barked. "I know what I'm doing!" The driver of the red Austin Healy got back in his car, and figured maybe the best thing for him to do was try and catch the others, and let them know what had happened.

Pulling Matt's jaw had triggered his fight-or-flight mechanism. Matt's brain sensed pain and started the body breathing to prepare for flight. And that's what Matt tried to do – get up and flee.

Harris was able to grab Matt in time, an open-field tackle, and use his own legs to wrap Matt's legs in a scissors grip, to keep him from getting up and running just like a wild animal into the woods where he certainly would have died. Mark Harris understood what was happening and he tried but simply couldn't hold Matt down by himself. Mark summoned Rudy and Chris to help, each holding a leg. Ken Gregory, the driver of the blue Porsche, grabbed a leg, too. "It was almost like a wrestling match," said Gregory. Matt was struggling to breath, gurgling blood, even as he fought to get up. Mary Ann Harris stayed by her husband, took off her jacket and placed it on top of Matt, to keep him warm. Rudy and Chris tried to speak to Matt – "You're going to be okay....You've got to go to medical school....your parents are coming" – but he was unresponsive. Rudy took off Matt's helmet. It was covered in blood.

They waited for the ambulance, holding Matt down, feeling his life slip away....

• • •

When Matt Miller left his apartment a little after 7:00 that morning, November 2, 2008, he was happier than he'd ever been in his life. Everything was coming together for the young man with a Hollywood jaw and 4.0 GPA. He was just a 20-year-old third-year student at the University of Virginia, but his path through life was so clear, so within his reach, all he had to do was live it. It had taken all of his 20 years to get to this point. But Matt Miller was nothing if not efficient and sensible. Figure out what you love and pursue it. All the pieces hadn't really come together until the last few months, and there still were a few hurdles ahead to clear – for instance, he had to graduate, and get into medical school, and get married – details like that. But that's what they were, only details. He had the plan and the will to make it happen. He was an exceptional young man with an exceptional future – just not the one he could foresee.

Matt was on his way that morning to meet Rudy and Chris. They were going to ride 85 miles into the Blue Ridge and up a mountain pass. As Matt pedaled through the silent, stunning Grounds of the University of Virginia, where almost every other student was still asleep, he had no reason to suspect that his beautiful future was about to be interrupted. It wasn't that Matt felt or believed he was invulnerable. It was just that vulnerability, at this moment in his life, was the furthest thing from his mind.

Honestly, if Matt had thought about it, if he had just stopped and looked at his life in perspective, he would have had to acknowledge that he'd just enjoyed the best week of his life. A big reason for that, of course, was Emily. Simply put, Matt Miller was in love with Emily Privette. He'd been in love with her since 8th grade, when he asked a friend of hers who sat next to him in the orchestra at Radnor Middle School in Pennsylvania to find out if she'd go with him to the 8th grade semi-formal. When he got word back that she'd say yes, he asked her. This, according to Matt, was about the only good thing ever to come from his playing the viola, but in the long run, well worth it. They separated much of the evening at the dance, as 13-year-olds do, to hang with their respective genders, but Matt always made sure to come find Emily for the slow dances. He asked her out on a real date after that – to see the latest *Star Wars* movie. Emily is the oldest of four, so this became an important family occasion. Her mother made a sign – "Emily's first date" – and forced Emily to hold it while she took a picture. Emily's little brothers even insisted on riding in the car with Emily and Matt to the movie. This was all a little too much for Emily. She wasn't one of those girls, "who ever since 6th grade had to have a boyfriend," she said, and she broke it off. But Matt never lost the torch. It wasn't until senior year at Radnor High School, when she felt he finally seemed to have lost interest in her, that she became totally interested in him. So high school! She started to instant message with him one evening – coincidentally, he will never forget, the day he got accepted early admission to Virginia. That was a great day. After a few more nights of *IM*ing, Matt knew a good thing and went for it, and asked Emily out to *Peace of Pizza* one night in early December of their senior year. They had been together ever since. Matt's attraction to Emily in middle school was the most basic – she was very pretty, with long brown hair, slender and lovely. And in high school and into college that never changed. But, again, Matt Miller was nothing if not sensible and practical. He knew a relationship built on looks alone could only last so long. Once they started dating, and got serious, she made him feel like he was somebody special, although he knew he was not. He did things for her, things he never did for anyone else, things he could never imagine himself ever doing, like writing her poetry, quoting her lyrics from pop songs. Sometimes around her he didn't recognize himself. Who was this guy? Plain and simple, Emily made him happy, and around her he felt like anything was possible. Matt long ago decided this was the girl he could marry.

And she was with him now at Virginia.

Matt remembered crying only a couple times in his whole 20 years of life. But one of them was after he dropped Emily off at the Philadelphia airport, when she flew off to start her first year of college at East Carolina University. They were going to be apart. Matt knew their relationship would endure, that this was true love, and Emily knew it too. But for Matt, a poet at heart, parting was sweet sorrow. He didn't actually let Emily see him cry. She was crying enough for both of them. But he cried in the car as he drove back to his family's home on the Philadelphia Main Line. He wouldn't be leaving for college, driving down to UVA, for another week. Matt and Emily drove back and forth between their universities – mostly Emily drove that first year, because Matt was on the UVA swim team, with practices every Saturday morning. And the second year of college was a little more even in the driving, but just as long and unsettled.

But Emily transferred to Virginia for her third year, and they were together, and after two years of not feeling quite settled, of things not feeling quite right, this most important piece of Matt's life – having Emily with him – was now in place and indescribably wonderful. After two months at UVA, Emily had adjusted well, made friends, felt increasingly at home. One reason this last week for Matt had been so great was that he and Emily on Thursday night, Halloween Eve, had gone to a dance party together. No more feeling awkward in another's college town, just a great night together, with friends.

The party was at a neighbor's house, out on the front lawn, with a live band. Matt and Emily enjoyed a little "pregaming" before the party began, but not too much, because Matt simply wasn't a boozer. He didn't need alcohol to feel good and serious drinking was just contrary to everything he believed. Getting drunk was so inefficient. He couldn't accept the idea of sleeping until 11:30 a.m. and waking up with a hangover. Your day would be gone. Your day would be wasted. He wasn't a prude or a scold. That lifestyle just made no sense for him. Because it was a Halloween party, Matt had dressed as a Frenchman, wearing a red beret and turtleneck, and Emily penciled in a thin, curlicue mustache making him quite the Bon Vivant. She went as a very un-matronly Mrs. Claus. Matt and Emily danced for hours under the stars. The evening was so relaxed, easy and fun. His heart was in tune.

That same week, on Tuesday, Matt and Emily had taken their first physics midterm, and aced it. And for both of them this was a huge step. Physics was the last hard science class standing in their way before they would apply to medical school the coming fall. And the class, clearly, was off to a good start.

Since the previous fall, for a full year, Matt had been shadowing the chief of general surgery at UVA hospital, John Hanks, at his weekly Wednesday clinic. Matt had also gone to the operating room on numerous occasions with Dr. Hanks, and had seen many patients come for pre-op appointments, surgery and post-op follow-ups. He'd blow the mind of the nurse practitioner working with Dr. Hanks, Ginny Simpson, not only by his dedication, coming week after week for a year – "I mean," she said, "how many undergraduates would do that?" – but also by his memory. Matt would remember these patients, and their stories. Ms. Simpson, as Matt always called her, would get furious with Dr. Hanks because he'd want to talk sports with Matt, whatever the season – "Hey, did you see the Phillies won three straight?" – and she couldn't stand to see patients wait because of boy banter. Not that she was anti-sports. She had season tickets to the Redskins. But she was old school. Patients came first. Matt was the one who'd tell Dr. Hanks, "We better keep moving, Ms. Simpson will get angry at you," and she loved Matt for that. Here he was the undergraduate, though everybody in the clinic just assumed he was already a medical student by the way he acted and how much he knew, trying to keep Hanks out of hot water with Ms. Simpson and the patients from having to wait.

If Matt wasn't sure he wanted to be a doctor before he followed Hanks around, he was certain after doing it for a year. He just couldn't think of a better way to spend his life, a more meaningful way. And what Hanks showed him, in addition to good doctoring, was that you could have a life outside of medicine. Hanks was devoted to his family, and also found time to exercise and follow sports. What impressed Matt most about Dr. Hanks, however, was his modesty. Hanks was one of America's leading endocrine surgeons. He was on national boards, a guy who'd accomplished so much, and yet he was so self-deprecating and humble around his patients, so able to put them at ease in the face of risky surgeries, and treat them with dignity and patience. If Hanks could display such modesty, Matt reasoned, then no doctor ever had any right to be arrogant.

In addition to his future spouse and his future profession, Matt had also discovered his dream sport – triathlons. For Matt, this was like early man discovering fire, or the wheel. It changed his life, and he was only now really just beginning to appreciate how much he loved this sport, how much he loved training and testing his own limits of endurance. Triathlons were one of the fastest-growing sports in the world, and Matt could have served as a poster child for its burgeoning popularity. He loved the variety of the three disciplines that make up a triathlon – swimming, biking and running, the challenge of being good at all three, of training for all three. Matt's affection for triathlons was very recent, only a few months, and the culmination of a search that began in college. When it came to triathlons, he was like a man wandering the desert who stumbled onto an oasis and plunged in.

During his first two years at Virginia, in addition to the absence of Emily, Matt had had another void in his life. He didn't have an activity outside of the classroom – a sport – which he could pour himself into. He'd always had one since he could remember – little league or golf or weight lifting or swimming – and he realized at college how important this was to him. A sport for Matt was more than just an outlet to let off steam, or a way to be part of a team. He was competitive. He thrived on competition. Not so much with others, as with himself. He needed a sport he could love and immerse himself in.

In high school, Matt swam on the Radnor high team. But, honestly, he was just following the path of his older brother. Matt had come to Virginia in his first year of college as a walk-on on the swim team, just as his brother, Michael, had done two years before him. Michael loved swimming, and ascended from walk-on to team captain in four years. But that was Michael Miller. Matt, two years behind his brother, just didn't love swimming as much, or feel he'd ever be successful enough, to stick with it. He really only joined the college team because the coach, Mark Bernardino, had asked him to join. Michael was such an asset, as a motivator and leader, even more than as a swimmer, and the coach figured Michael's little brother would be as well.

So Matt walked on freshman year like his brother. But the truth is swim team in his first year of college became a chore to Matt. He gave it his best every day, his absolute best, because that was who he was. But he didn't look forward to it. He didn't love it. His sport, his activity, was out there waiting for him to discover. So after one season of swimming in college, he decided to walk away.

When he was on the UVA swim team that one year, Matt was nicknamed *Sleeves*. This was because he always wore sleeveless shirts, showing off his biceps. In fact, the nickname was coined the day he cut off the sleeves on his sweatshirt. Who does that? The boy was not without his youthful vanities. The theory was that Matt had been a chubby little boy, though he will claim he was never chubby, but just had a little extra baby fat. So in high school he really began pumping iron. Maybe it was to impress girls, or catch Emily's eye. At the same time in high school, he became obsessed with eating right. He gave up all sweets and sodas, began to bake his own "Vitamuffins" and even refused to eat cake on his own birthday, though his mother always baked one for the rest of the family.

After he quit the swim team at Virginia, he continued his love affair with the weight room. At the beginning of his second year of college, he started showing up every morning at 6:00 at the main recreation center on Grounds.

While Matt was good at lifting weights, and loved the look, he realized that this wasn't the outlet he was looking for. He was never going to be nor did he want to be a professional body builder, yet he wanted something he could compete in, something he could dedicate himself to. So that winter he decided to start running. Matt had always hated to run, certainly anything more than a 40-yard dash. In youth soccer he'd always been the goalie because he hated to run, and as a swimmer he'd always been a sprinter. He couldn't even endure the thought of an endurance event. But he wanted to stay in shape, and he was on a mission of exploration. Amazingly, Matt found he was pretty good at running, and even enjoyed it. He started training in the mornings, and signed up for a couple of 10ks (6.2 milers), and even a half marathon, 13.1 miles, running that in one hour and thirty-six minutes – very good considering how little training he had done.

Matt's father was telling some of his coworkers about Matt's new affection for running. Mike Miller, Matt's dad, was a managing director at Vanguard, the mutual fund giant located in Malvern, outside of Philadelphia. (Matt's dad went by Mike, and his brother by Michael.) To know Mike Miller was really to know his sons, or feel like you knew them, because he just loved them so much and enjoyed them so much and was so proud of them and so often shared stories about them. He didn't do this in a boastful way, but an exuberant one. Sometimes his wife, Nancy, would just roll her eyes, because she was raised in Roanoke, Virginia, by parents who believed you never talked about yourself or your children and their accomplishments because it might make somebody else feel uncomfortable. She was high school valedictorian and somebody "leaked" (her word) the news to the pastor and her parents were just mortified when he announced the accomplishment to the entire congregation. In Nancy Miller's world, that just wasn't done. But Mike was Mike and he loved his boys.

One of Mike Miller's colleagues, Tim Buckley, 40, for whom Mike had been a mentor, suggested to Mike that Matt should get a bicycle and consider triathlons. Buckley said that with Matt's swimming and running ability, he would be a natural triathlete. Buckley didn't really know Matt, only through Mike's stories, but said he'd be happy to help Matt pick out a road bike. Matt had never thought about triathlons, or ridden a road bike, but he was on a mission of exploration, and this sounded good to him. So that June, between his second and third years of college, Matt came home and Tim Buckley helped him choose a bike.

Emily named it Black Beauty.

From the moment Matt got on Black Beauty, he knew, almost like he knew from the very beginning that Emily was the right girl for him. He just loved the bike.

Pretty soon, in mid-June, Matt was riding with Buckley and some of his Vanguard colleagues, Chris McIsaac and Colin Kelton, and even Bill McNabb, the Vanguard CEO, on morning rides before work. Matt was a college kid, home for the summer. Yet he thought nothing of meeting these executives at the Main Line YMCA parking lot by 5:15 a.m., so they could ride 20 miles and be at their desks by 7:30. And of course Matt was the one guy wearing the reflector vest, so concerned about safety. On their first ride together, the Vanguard crew literally had to begin by teaching Matt how to clip in and out of his pedals. These men were all amazed at how good Matt got and how fast he got there.

For most people it takes years to develop the stamina and strength to be a good cyclist. But from years of swimming, and now a year of running, and because he must have been blessed with good genes, Matt turned out to be a cardio vascular machine. On summer Saturdays Matt and the Vanguard crew would go for 60-mile circuit rides, out to French Creek State Park in the far Philadelphia suburbs. On their first French Creek ride, Matt crested the nastiest hill right with Buckley, a phenomenal biker, who pointed out that Matt's thighs were quivering, in spasm. Buckley asked if Matt were OK.

"It's going to take a lot more to break me," Matt told him.

In August, Matt and his family went on vacation for two weeks to Wintergreen, in the Blue Ridge Mountains, about an hour from Charlottesville, and Matt brought Black Beauty and every day rode up and down the main road of Wintergreen Mountain, a ski resort. Matt hated the downhill, it terrified him, but he relished the climbing, pushing himself and then pushing himself harder. He simply loved the bike. He was never going to be Lance

Armstrong, but he sensed with his swimming background, his potential as a runner, and his rapidly increasing stamina on the bike, he could really excel at triathlons. He also loved the variety. He could cross train without injury, or boredom, and he could really begin to test his own limits, which he found is what he loved most of all.

That September, back at UVA to begin his third year, Matt traveled to Virginia Beach to compete in his first big triathlon, a relatively short one known as the Sandman. It began with a 2/3-mile swim in the Atlantic Ocean, followed by 14 miles on the bike, and ended with a three-mile run. Matt finished fourth out of 465 men and was second-fastest on the bike leg – averaging 26 miles per hour.

He'd been training on the bike for three months.

———

CHAPTER TWO

M ary Ann Harris felt like the ambulance would never arrive.
  "I thought it was an eternity," she said.
  "It felt like forever," said Rudy.
  "It got there quickly," said Mark Harris.
  R.W. Woody was a good old country boy, from the mountains of central
Virginia, with a voice as seasoned and smooth and southern as an old piece
of hickory wood. He was 44, riding on ambulances since he was 16, when
he used to go out on calls with his granddaddy. He was now a state certi-
fied medic and firefighter, the shift captain on duty at Wintergreen Fire and
Rescue. He was relaxing in an old comfy lounge chair, nearly three hours
into his 24-hour shift, watching some bad Sunday morning TV when the
call came in.
  Usually at that time of year, early November, about the worst calls they
got were for bee stings – bees get aggressive with hikers when the weather
starts to get cold. R.W. and his colleagues were a professional staff, on duty
24/7, year round, because they were located at Wintergreen Ski Resort, which
was really a year-round community now, with condos and a golf course as
well as a ski mountain. Where R.W. happened to be sitting in his lounger
wasn't much more than five miles by ambulance from where Matt Miller lay
on the pavement.
  At the time, the Wintergreen Fire and Rescue was the only professional,
fulltime, on-duty rescue squad covering the Blue Ridge Parkway within 100
miles. Frankly, it was the only professional squad covering the Parkway all

the way down to the North Carolina line. If that accident had happened anywhere else, if that call had come into a volunteer rescue squad, the volunteers likely would have been in church on this Sunday morning, or in their homes, and would have had to get to their ambulance location, load and go. No telling how much longer that would have taken. And in trauma, especially with brain injuries, every moment matters.

R.W. got the call from Augusta County dispatch at 10:44 a.m. Lights flashed and alarms rang inside the rescue squad building. There was no chance anyone sleeping during a 24 hour shift could miss the alarm.

R.W.'s partner was on the toilet.

"I'll be there in a little bit," his partner shouted.

That wouldn't do. This wasn't any bee sting. The call came in as "motor vehicle crash involving a bike."

"Drop it," R.W. yelled. "Pinch it and run."

But his partner needed a few more minutes and R.W. couldn't wait. R.W. was in the ambulance and on his way in less than two minutes. He was at the scene by 10:52.

When he arrived, R.W. had this feeling, there's no other way to describe it – "Oh, shit!" This was what he called an "Oh, shit!" call. The worst. Here was this boy, his face smashed like a pumpkin, lying in the road, and this man holding him down. The man – Harris – looked to R.W. as if he'd been in a fight, his clothes were so red, so bloody. R.W. saw the mangled bike still in the road and the banged up sports car off to the side. The boy was thrashing about so that R.W. was sure he had massive brain injuries. That's what people do with brain injuries. And here R.W. was by himself. First thing he did, after thinking "Oh, shit!" was get on his little 10-watt portable hand-held radio and call for the helicopter. This boy would need medical evacuation. But of course, just like Rudy had trouble getting reception on his cellphone, R.W.'s hand-held radio didn't have enough power to hit the repeaters, which were blocked by the high ridge at that very spot. He hustled back to his ambulance, which had a much more powerful 100-watt radio, and called dispatch. "We need Aircare 5. Send them to Reeds Gap." He ran back to the man and the boy. The man, Harris, asked him a little gruffly, "Where's everybody else?" "I got some people comin,'" R.W. replied.

R.W. stayed calm and went to work. He remembered his training – the ABCs – airway, breathing and circulation. He never really got past the airway. Matt was gasping. R.W. put an oxygen mask on the boy, and tried to suction out blood. He got back on his radio, and spoke directly to the helicopter crew. "He's having major airway problems and he's combative." R.W. got a cervical spine collar and backboard out of his ambulance. First thing Mark Harris did was tell R.W. that he was a physician, and R.W. was grateful to have the help. With the assistance of Harris, Rudy and Chris, R.W. log-rolled Matt carefully onto the board, strapped him down, and put on the cervical spine collar. R.W. started two IVs, one in each arm, the biggest gauge tubing he had, just running saline. That's all he was licensed to do. Soon enough his colleague from the toilet arrived in a fire engine, standard procedure when an automobile is involved. One never knew if there would be gasoline leaks, fire, even an explosion. And then two more volunteers from the golf course rescue station down the mountain arrived, and National Park Service Rangers who closed the road. The rangers would close the road for three hours, interviewing all the witnesses and measuring all the distances, even reconstructing the accident, doing an exceptionally thorough investigation because they were sure this would be a fatality.

R.W. told the volunteers to take the fire truck to Reeds Gap, to inspect the landing zone for the helicopter. That was also procedure. The helicopter wouldn't land without an inspection and a fire truck there. R.W. and his partner now put Matt on the gurney, loaded him into the ambulance and started back 1.5 miles to Reeds Gap. It was 11:09 when they pulled away. R.W. said 17 minutes at the scene might sound like a long time, but it was a flat out sprint. He had done his best for this young man, the little good he expected it to do.

• • •

That fall, for his third year of college, Matt had moved back into a duplex with friends on Montebello Circle, less than a mile from the central Grounds. A group of girls that August moved into the other half of the duplex, and pretty quickly that semester, Matt had befriended one of them, Carrie Barnes, a nursing student. She knew him only as *Sleeves*, because that's what everyone called him. In fact, she put his number into her cell phone as Sleeves.

That fall, knowing Carrie only a few weeks, Matt asked her a big favor. He put it directly, the only way Matt can, so honest as to be almost old fashioned. Emily had just transferred to Virginia, and Matt asked Carrie if she would show Emily the ropes, include her in Carrie's circle of girlfriends, and help with Emily's transition. Carrie was happy to help out. And the request turned out to be a wonderful gift. In just a couple months, Emily and Carrie became the best of friends. Pretty soon Emily was a regular at Girls Night on Tuesdays at Carrie's house, where all the girls gathered to drink wine and watch *The Hills*, a reality show.

At the same time, Carrie did a favor for Matt. She saw that fall that he was into training for triathlons. Carrie had gone to James River High School outside Richmond with Rudy Kahsar, also a UVA student. Carrie would often see Rudy over at the UVA pool, where she worked as a lifeguard, when the pool would be open for general lap swimming. Carrie told Matt, "I have to introduce you to my friend Rudy. You guys would be perfect together." Rudy happened to be president of the UVA triathlon club. Rudy had run cross country in high school, and swam on a summer swim team growing up, but he savored the biking leg most of all. He had spent his first two years at UVA, and now into his third, training and touring all through central Virginia, riding up into the Blue Ridge Mountains and even on occasion down the other side, into the Shenandoah Valley.

Rudy and Matt began training together often that fall. Rudy was the one who suggested the 85-mile ride that Sunday morning, November 2. Rudy planned the route and had ridden variations of it many times before.

The day before their big ride, that Saturday, Matt invited Rudy to go to brunch with him and his family at the Boar's Head Inn, which had an

awesome buffet. With all the calories these boys were burning on their training rides together, Rudy's eyes lit up at the invitation.

Matt's brother, Michael, who had graduated and was now a first-year
student at Stanford Law School, had flown back to Charlottesville for the
weekend because he was being honored at halftime of the football game,
along with the rest of the previous year's swim team, for winning the Atlantic
Coast Conference championship. Matt's parents, Mike and Nancy Miller,
who also had gone to UVA and met as undergraduates, had flown down
from Philadelphia for the weekend and the chance to be with both of their
sons. Matt's grandparents even drove up from Roanoke. It was at brunch on
Saturday at the Boar's Head Inn that Matt told his parents he wouldn't be
able to meet them on Sunday, before they flew home, because he had this
wonderful ride planned with his new triathlon friend, Rudy.

Matt went to the football game that Saturday afternoon to watch
the swim team ceremony. It was also a big game, against the powerhouse
University of Miami, and Virginia had the game won until they fumbled
it away in overtime. Matt was barely paying attention to the game. He was
much more excited about the next day's ride. The weekend before, he'd completed a 100-mile charity ride around Charlottesville – riding 30 of those
miles alongside a pro cyclist. This had been such a thrill for him, to keep
pace with a pro. As Matt and the girls sat on the hill behind the end zone,
in the student section, he kept telling Emily and Carrie about the next day's
ride, and where they were headed, and how many feet of total elevation they
would be climbing. And of course each time the girls just rolled their eyes.
Matt and his workouts. Matt and his training. Carrie had come to believe Emily
was the perfect match for Matt, providing levity to balance out his intensity,
a little disorder to his order.

• • •

After R.W. Woody pulled away in the ambulance, Mark Harris said to Rudy,
"You need to reach that boy's parents." It was no surprise that Mark Harris
was the calmest one there, thinking the most clearly. He'd been a doctor for

over 30 years. And of course he had children of his own. He was thinking like a doctor and a parent.

Matt almost always rode with his cell phone. But on that morning, because he knew Rudy would be carrying a phone, Matt left his phone at home. Extra weight. That was just like Matt. Rudy's mind started racing. He knew Matt's parents, visiting UVA for the weekend, would be heading to the airport, flying back to Philly around noon. He had to reach them before they left. But how?

Emily would be able to reach Matt's parents, but Rudy did not have Emily's number in his cell phone. Carrie Barnes could surely reach Emily, but for some reason Rudy didn't even have Carrie's number in his phone, even though he'd gone to high school *and* college with her. He forced himself to stay calm. *Think, Rudy, Think.* Rudy had a chemical engineering classmate, Marcel, whose number he did have in his phone, and Rudy knew that Marcel lived on Montebello Circle, not far from Carrie and Matt. Marcel didn't know Carrie or Matt, and he was going to think Rudy was crazy, but Rudy knew this was the only way.

He climbed back high on those rocks, with his miraculous one bar, and reached Marcel. Rudy was crying, and he knows he must have scared the you-know-what out of Marcel, but he told him, "I know this sounds crazy, but you've got to go down to that duplex, and knock on the door, and ask for Carrie, and tell her Matt's been hurt, really bad, and she needs to reach his parents. Tell them the helicopter's coming and he's going to be flown to UVA."

Carrie, a third year nursing student, was in her room studying for a big anatomy test. She had told herself she was going to study all day Sunday. She almost never studied in her room, although that morning, of all mornings, heaven knows why, she decided to study at her desk. Her roommate knocked on her door and told her there was this strange guy at the front door and he was trembling and said he had to talk to Carrie, that Matt had been in a bad accident. Carrie got up and as she went downstairs she couldn't for the life of her imagine who this guy could have been or who he would have been talking about. Who was Matt?

The student at the door truly was shaking. He blurted out, "I need to speak to Carrie. Rudy just called me to tell you that Matt got into a bad accident."

Carrie was still just plain puzzled. "Matt? Matt?"

Finally her roommate said to her, "Matt *Miller.*"

A wave of realization and dread washed over Carrie. Just like a slap. *Sleeves.* In a flash she was out the door, and in her car, to go get Emily. Carrie was terrified about telling Emily this horrible news, this was immediately the hardest thing she'd ever had to do in her life, but she had to do it. Carrie understood she had to get word to Matt's parents before they flew home, and Emily would be the only one to know how to do that. She called Emily on the phone and told her to stay calm that she was coming to see her that she had bad news to tell her but didn't want to tell her over the phone. And Emily tried to give Carrie directions to her dorm, Gooch, which was actually only five minutes away but of course Carrie couldn't find Emily's dorm. Emily lived in dorms for transfer students, high up on Observatory Hill, where nobody who ever actually started at Virginia as a first-year student ever went or even knew about, and even though Emily tried to give Carrie directions Carrie couldn't find it. So Carrie finally just told Emily on the phone, stay calm, don't freak out, don't panic, but Matt's been in a bad accident and he's being flown by helicopter to UVA hospital. Now of course Emily did freak out and started crying, and she would be the first one to tell you that she's emotional, and no one would ever accuse her of being the strong silent type. And she was frantic and she just couldn't wait for Carrie to try and find her dorm so she just started running to Carrie's house. So she was running and crying, crying and running, through the Grounds of the University, and people were staring at her and thinking who was this crazy girl but she didn't care, and she got to Carrie's house just as Carrie was pulling up and the two girls hugged and sobbed and Carrie calmed Emily down and told her she had to call Matt's parents right away.

• • •

After he called Marcel, Rudy just stood there, in the middle of the road, and thought to himself, "Now what? What do we do?" It had been so hectic and loud, so urgent and frantic, and now it was so quiet. Rudy and Chris just went over to the side of the road and sat in the grass. "This changes everything," Rudy said to himself. Chris felt the same way. Everything had been a blur, dizzying, with no time to think. And now, for the first time, with the ambulance gone, both boys began to process what they'd just seen and experienced, what it meant. Both Rudy and Chris were pretty sure Matt was going to die. They suddenly had this overwhelming appreciation for the preciousness of life, and felt this hammer blow, this crushing realization of just how quickly and suddenly this precious gift can be gone. They just sat there, a mess, mostly in silence. Their cycling clothes and hands were bloody.

Mark and Mary Ann Harris walked over to them. The boys asked Dr. Harris if Matt would be okay, and he told them he didn't know. But he was thinking to himself that the young man wouldn't reach the hospital alive. That's what he told his wife. It's not that Mark Harris was a cynic or pessimist. He just knew how things were. He had experience with death and with dying patients. Mary Ann Harris, who had been a career social worker, tried to comfort the boys, and also walked over to check on Ken Gregory, to see if he was all right. After the initial few moments, when he helped keep Matt under control, Ken Gregory had drifted off to the other side of the road, and was just standing by his car, his blue Porsche, dazed. Mary Ann believed he was in shock. "I couldn't do anything," he mumbled to her. "He just came at me." Mary Ann believed she knew how Ken felt, and felt the same way herself. Looking at Matt lying in the road, she couldn't help but feel this immense and overwhelming sense of loss and despair. This fabulous treasure – a young man's future – had just been stolen. Mary Ann felt like an accomplice. She had watched it happen. Matt would surely die or never be the same, whichever was worse.

They could all hear the helicopter now, getting ready to land up at Reeds Gap. Rudy's cell phone rang. It was Carrie. He scurried back toward the boulders so he could hear. She wanted to know more but he didn't know much more. It was bad. Real bad.

. . .

When he had started the bike ride that Sunday morning, Matt knew it was going to be a spectacular autumn day, reaching into the low 60s, with sunny skies and almost no wind, a flat-out perfect day for cycling. He was wearing gloves, and booties over his bike shoes, protection from the morning chill, but knew he'd shed them later on as he warmed up. He could see his breath as he pedaled to the football stadium parking lot, to rendezvous with Rudy and Chris. Chris, 21, a fourth-year student from Baltimore, had just that week accepted a job after graduation with an economics consulting firm in Washington D.C., so he saw spending a beautiful day on the bike as a celebration and reward. Chris was a superb swimmer – and had swum all through high school with the North Baltimore Aquatics Club, and was in the same workout group as Olympic champion Michael Phelps, to give some idea of the company he kept. But he chose not to swim in college so he could focus on academics and other interests. And one interest soon became triathlons. In the summer between high school and college, Chris decided to enter the Great Chesapeake Bay Swim, a 4.4-mile race underneath the Chesapeake Bay Bridge, along with about 800 competitors. He won. That was how his interest in endurance events and triathlons was born. In the last few years, he'd competed in about ten triathlons, even a half Ironman, which included a 56-mile bike ride, but biking was by far his weakest leg. He'd taken long rides before – but never up a mountain. Chris was a member of the UVA triathlon club and actually first met Matt at the triathlon in Virginia Beach (Chris had finished 12th to Matt's 4th). Chris was looking forward to a great day with Rudy and Matt, excited about getting out into the countryside on his bike, but he did have some trepidation about the mountain climb.

The three riders had headed west out of Charlottesville, the sun rising behind them, the golden rays coming in at the gentlest angles and falling on the most magnificent countryside. They felt so utterly blessed and fortunate, so energized and ready to go. This ride was in some ways a perfect metaphor for their lives – just taking off, with mountains to climb. This was a moment in life to freeze the frame, when life just can't get any better. These three young men were going to ride 85 miles through paradise. With the hubris of youth, they were going to scale a mountain pass. They were so fit. So perfect. So ready.

They sliced through the heart of the university that Thomas Jefferson founded and designed, and headed west. Two miles out of town they could already see the marvelous Blue Ridge, ablaze in fall foliage still, just 30 miles away. They pedaled past miles of white picket fences and perfectly manicured horse farms with red brick mansions. These young men were training, not touring, but they were well aware of how beautiful their surroundings were, how much it added to their enjoyment. On rides like this Rudy often felt like he was in on a secret that few other students ever knew, because they rarely lost themselves in the countryside, as he did. And the boys were having fun. When they would ride by a particularly beautiful or impressive estate, one of them would shout out to the others, "I wonder who lives in *that* one."

About 9:45 a.m., 45 miles into the ride, they began the climb to Reeds Gap, elevation 2,654 above sea level. This was the climb they'd all been waiting for. Reeds Gap is a mountain pass on the Blue Ridge Parkway, the point where county road 664 rises up and intersects from the east. The climb to Reeds Gap rises about 2,000 feet in just 5.5 miles. Were they riding in the Tour de France, this would be considered a category one climb – among the toughest.

Rudy, in the lead, just started pedaling up the county road, followed by Matt, and then Chris. The climb starts out slowly, tantalizingly easily, in fact. But if they looked up, each of them could see the ski slopes of Wintergreen resort high above, whose entrance they would be passing. Each knew what was coming. Within half a mile of beginning the climb, each rider was out of his saddle, standing on his pedals, pumping, in the easiest gear, pumping, pumping, pumping, sweating, and pumping.

Their line thinned out, Rudy distancing himself from Matt, and Matt from Chris. Each was not in competition with the other, but with himself. The mountain was throwing everything it could at them, including a quarter-mile-long straightaway rising at an incline of 16 degrees. That feels like straight up to a cyclist – no curves, no breaks, just up. Yet each kept climbing.

Matt had discovered in these months of endurance training, especially climbing these mountains, that the mind gives out long before the body, and
the challenge, the essential element of endurance training, is to convince the
mind not to quit, to continue, that the body can persist and must be pushed
along. For these riders, the pain was intense, particularly in their thighs and
in their guts, their lungs heaving, but that's what they wanted. They wanted
to find their limit and expand it. Steady. Steady. As they neared the sum-
mit, they were drenched in sweat but also in euphoria. Rudy crested the
mountain pass first, followed by Matt, 200 yards behind, and Chris another
few hundred yards behind Matt. It was a moment of triumph. Rudy cheered
Matt, and Matt and Rudy cheered Chris. They got off their bikes to take
long drinks and also to drink in what they'd accomplished. Each boy was
in every sense on top of the world. There was nobody else around. Just sky
and wind and their pounding hearts. The triathletes drank generously and
leisurely, ate an energy bar, and high-fived one another in celebration. For
Matt Miller, at that very moment, he felt he could overcome any challenge
that life presented.

• • •

When Mark Harris was 14, growing up in York, Pennsylvania, his mother,
who loved everything British, bought a 1953 red MG sports car. Her plan
was to drive it for a year or two, and when Mark got his license, he could
drive it to and from high school because she was tired of driving him. Pretty
quickly she decided this car wasn't for a suburban mom, and went back to
her station wagon. Mark didn't wait, however, and, despite being underage,
drove it all around the back roads of York County whenever his parents were
away. And at age 16, once licensed, he indeed drove it to school. He also
took it apart and rebuilt it and somehow over the next 45 years Mark Harris
acquired five more MGs, a Ferrari, Mercedes and a gorgeous 1965 Pontiac
GTO. And he still had that 1953 MG. He'd had a romance with that car even
longer than with his wife, Mary Ann, whom he met while in high school,

married after college, and was now, on the morning of November 2, about to take on a beautiful foliage ride with the Shenandoah Valley British Car Club.

Mark Harris, 60, was an anesthesiologist at Martha Jefferson Hospital in Charlottesville, and he managed to squeeze his seven sports cars in an expanded two-car garage. He didn't drive any of them very often, but as his own kids were grown now, he loved devoting his weekends to his cars, tinkering with them, taking them on small trips. He regularly rotated the cars in his garage, to give them all equal time on the road, and for this drive, for the simple reason that it was in front of the line, he chose a white 1970 MGB GT.

The car club that day was meeting up on Afton Mountain, right at milepost 0 of the Blue Ridge Parkway. The road, a two-lane ribbon in the sky, stretches 469 miles from the Shenandoah National Park in Virginia to the Great Smoky Mountains National Park in North Carolina. It runs along the crest of the Blue Ridge Mountains. This is not a road anyone takes to get somewhere in a hurry. It is a road for tourists and touring, and the maximum speed limit, for good and obvious reasons, is 45 miles per hour. On this particular morning, the objective of the British Car Club was to drive south on the Parkway and have lunch at the Peaks of Otter Lodge, at milepost 86.

About 30 cars assembled in the parking lot on Afton Mountain. All of them were classics, and breakdowns were not uncommon. Even though he had been coming to these car rallies for many years, Mark Harris had never been asked by club organizers to ride "Sweeper" – until now. The sweeper's job was to be the last car in the caravan, the caboose, and help any club member who might break down. The club president gave Mark a walkie-talkie, and if a problem occurred, Mark was to radio ahead to the club president, who would be the lead car. Although Mark hadn't done any engine work to speak of in years, he was agreeable but a little uncomfortable being the sweeper.

Mark and Mary Ann were friendly with another member of the club, Ken Gregory. Ken, 59, was from Massachusetts, north of Boston. Ken also had always loved cars. He owned eight sports cars, two BMW motorcycles, and a truck. After 30 years of being a "flying screwdriver," traveling all the time, installing and fixing things – electronic cash registers in the 1970s, new scanning systems in the 1980s, and debit and credit card systems in the 1990s – Ken just got tired of flying after 9/11. He knew a guy from the antique car world who ran a body shop near Waynesboro, Virginia, halfway up on the west side of Afton Mountain. The man had often said to Ken if you move down here, I'll give you a job. So Ken, who'd been rebuilding and repairing cars all his life out of love, relocated to the Waynesboro area and began his semi-retirement working three days a week in the man's repair shop.

That's where Ken met Mark Harris, a regular customer.

Ken had just bought his 1972 Porsche 911T (T is for touring) a few weeks earlier. He bought it in part because of the color – Mexico Blue – as beautiful as any water, just a joyous rich shimmering blue. The car was a bargain at $15,000, worth at least $30,000. The last thing Ken Gregory needed or was looking for was another car, but at least he knew he wouldn't lose money on this one. And not only did he love the color, but this car was a "survivor" – never in an accident, never rebuilt, repaired or repainted. More than 36 years old and still original. Even though this was the Shenandoah Valley *British* Car Club, Ken drove his German-built Porsche that morning because he wanted to try it out. The Parkway twists and turns, rises and falls, a fun, fun place to drive.

When Ken heard that Mark Harris was riding sweeper, he offered to hang back with him, just in case anybody actually broke down and needed help. Mark was appreciative. So a little after 10:00 a.m., the classic car caravan pulled out, heading south, expecting a peaceful and pleasant drive to lunch. Ken Gregory was the second to last car out of the parking lot, followed by Mark and Mary Ann Harris.

• • •

After taking several minutes to celebrate and recover from the climb, Rudy, Matt and Chris set out on the rest of their journey. The hardest and longest part of the ride was now over. The trio expected to enjoy an easy, rolling ride north on the Parkway for roughly 14 miles, and when they reached the intersection with highway 250, atop Afton Mountain, the riders would turn east, head down the mountain on Route 250, and almost literally glide back home to Charlottesville. For this next stretch of the ride, northbound on the Parkway, they were going to do what Rudy described as a pace line. The leader pulls the trio along, and when he's ready for a break, he "falls off" toward the center of the lane as the next two riders stay in their line and "pull through" on the outside of the lane, closest to the shoulder. The former leader drops in behind them, now at the rear of the line.

A mile or so after resuming their ride, the trio began to see these classic British sports cars coming toward them, and passing by them, in the southbound lane. The bikers could not help but notice, and would remark to one another as a particularly cool car would pass. Traffic was the last thing any one of the cyclists was concerned with. Even though the road was a winding two-lane, with no paved shoulder, cars were infrequent. Not one had yet to pass the bikers going in their own northbound direction since they had reached Reeds Gap. This was a training ride for them, not a touring ride, so they were still working pretty hard, but they were young men and these were sports cars and it was only natural to take a look, especially since the riders were in such a good mood and feeling so triumphant.

And then...

Between 10:35 and 10:40 a.m., Rudy, riding in the lead, heard a noise behind him.

As best he can describe, it was the noise of somebody struggling. "I turned around," he said, "just in time to see Matt in the middle of the road." Matt was perpendicular to the double yellow line, and falling. Rudy didn't see the actual impact, because he had to turn back around to keep his own balance. But he heard it, a sickening thud.

Most cyclists improve their technique, and their skill handling the bike, as they improve their endurance. By the time they're taking 85-mile rides, they've ridden many miles and learned how to ride in formation, how to turn their heads – glancing behind them or to the side – while keeping in control of their bikes, keeping them straight and in formation. But Matt was different, Rudy felt. Matt had this amazing cardiovascular system – his resting heart rate, for crying out loud, was 42! – and he could bike up mountains almost from the first day he clipped in. So riding 85 miles, even up a mountain pass, was something Matt was able to do relatively quickly. But Matt still didn't have much experience as a cyclist – just five months. This is the only way Rudy could explain what happened. He believed Matt, looking at the Porsche, or one of the other cars, must have rolled off the crown of the pavement, onto the dirt shoulder, overcompensated, lost control, and swerved – like a broadside torpedo hit – into the oncoming Porsche.

Chris actually saw it happen. Chris was in the rear, his head down, pedaling, but he saw Matt start to lose control of his bike. He saw Matt's handlebars begin to wobble. Chris can't explain what caused it. Rudy was riding far enough in front of Matt, and Chris far enough behind, so that neither of their bikes clipped Matt's wheels, which would have caused him to lose control. Chris did notice there was debris in the road, sticks and such, and maybe Matt had hit a stone or a stick with his thin front tire and lost his balance. Whatever the cause, Chris sensed something was wrong, and looked up to see Matt's handlebars teetering from side to side. Chris saw Matt overcompensate, overcorrect, swerve across his lane and cross the yellow line. Matt was falling directly into the oncoming Porsche. Honestly, to Chris, everything seemed to be in slow motion. Chris could see the inevitability of it all just before it happened. He saw Matt toppling forward. He saw the blue Porsche, almost even with Matt now. Chris hoped it would have time to veer to its right, avoiding the falling rider, but the driver didn't have time to react. Chris was sure he saw Matt's face hit the left front headlight and fender.

Upon impact, Matt Miller and Black Beauty flew into the air, flipped, and landed in the southbound lane, near the yellow line, at milepost 12.2. Matt lay motionless in the road, still clipped into his bicycle pedals.

• • •

Ken Gregory was enjoying the ride, and the feel of his new car. Around Milepost 12, a long and unusual straightaway, he saw the bikers. They were coming toward him, in the opposite lane, so he had a good long look. He could tell they were booking it, moving at a good clip. They had their heads down, low on the handlebars, not like tourists. They were wearing bright cycling clothes, helmets. He was cruising along at about 40 miles per hour.

Right as he was about to pass them by, with his peripheral vision, he thought he saw the second rider pulling out toward the middle, as if to pass the first rider. At least that's what it looked like to him. It all happened so fast. He thought the second rider somehow jerked his wheel too fast, too far, causing the bike and the rider to flip right over the handle bar. Ken did some motorcycling in his day, and he had heard of that happening sometimes with a motorcycle. He called it high-siding. The accident happened in a split second, but Ken was pretty sure the second rider's face slammed right into his windshield post – the steel post that supports the windshield on the driver's side. "It was pretty horrifying," he said.

Instinctively, Ken jerked the steering wheel, but it was too late. The collision had already occurred. He swerved right, into the grass, and lost control of his car for a moment. Luckily for him, this was one of the widest stretches of the Parkway, a straightaway, and there was a strip of grass between the road and the trees and precipice. He felt for an instant that he was going to die, too, that his car was out of control and would go flying into the trees. An experienced driver, Ken knew enough not to slam on his brakes in the grass. And after that second of being out of control, he managed to regain control of his car, and stopped as quickly as he could. He got out of the car, and ran back to the second rider, whom he was sure he had just killed. Mark Harris was already there.

———

CHAPTER THREE

Robin Root was 53, old for a flight nurse. He'd worked as an emergency room nurse most of his career, but this was the best job he'd ever had. Two years before, in 2006, he was the last person hired for a new medical evacuation team being formed in the Shenandoah Valley, which was underserved. The helicopter was based in Weyers Cave, right along Interstate 81, in the heart of the Valley. For him, this was a calling, not a profession. He had discovered that there was no better feeling in the world than saving a life. He had delivered babies, and seen his own babies born. But responding to a trauma, saving a life in a crisis, getting an accident victim to a hospital in time – it was hard to describe how worthwhile that could make a person feel.

The call came in from dispatch, "bike versus car." Only two places along the first 25 miles of the Blue Ridge Parkway were wide enough for a helicopter to land – milepost 5.7 at Humpback Rocks, and milepost 13.7, Reeds Gap.

Aircare 5, as Root's team was known, was never dispatched until the first responder on the scene, in this case, R.W. Woody, summoned them. The longer it took to get a first responder to the scene, the longer it took to get the helicopter in the air. As it was, the call came in to Aircare 5 at 10:57. The decision by the pilot to fly, that conditions were acceptable (fog on the mountain can often be a consideration), was made by 10:58. It took six minutes to prep the helicopter. The flight was about 25 nautical miles. Robin Root touched down at Reeds Gap at 11:19. The ambulance had been waiting only a few moments.

The pilot stayed on board, keeping the chopper "hot," rotors whirring and ready for departure. There were two medical professionals on board – Robin, the flight nurse, and a medic. They knew what they would be facing so on the flight over they got their drugs drawn, their equipment ready. Each had a specific job.

They ran to the ambulance. The first thing Robin noticed was Matt's face. "His face was just mashed," he recalled. The second thing he noticed was how much difficulty Matt was having trying to breath.

Brent Henyon, the medic with Robin, first set up monitors on the patient – for blood pressure, pulse, and blood oxygen – then immediately began to push drugs through the IV. These were immensely powerful drugs, first a paralytic, then a sedative. The paralytic did just that, paralyzed Matt, stopped him from moving, even stopped him from breathing. It took effect in less than a minute. But just in case Matt – or any patient – would have been alert, or conscious, that paralytic wouldn't have dulled the senses. A patient would have been fully aware he couldn't breath and couldn't move and it would have been inhuman, if not torture, to paralyze a patient without sedating him as well, knocking him out. Matt needed to be immobilized both for his own safety, and also so that Robin Root could make the money shot, could do what he'd been trained to do, put a breathing tube down Matt's throat, into his trachea, and open an airway. Matt was no longer breathing on his own, the paralytic had worked perfectly, so the pressure was on Robin Root to do this right, and do it quick.

First, Robin took a tool that looked like a shoe horn, but much more medical in terminology and function, and pried open Matt's throat, lifting everything floating around out of the way. The shoe horn had a light on it, but there was really not much to see that made sense – everything was out of place. But so much of what Robin did anyway was based on feel. Robin slid the tube perfectly down into the trachea, which connects to the lungs, and then began bagging– pushing oxygen into the lungs manually – until he and the medic could wheel Matt's gurney from the ambulance into the helicopter, which Robin described as an "Emergency Room with a rotor." It had a mechanical ventilator on board, and at that point, the machine started doing the breathing for Matt.

Matt Miller was strapped into the Eurocopter 135 and airborne by 11:37, one hour, perhaps to the minute, after his accident. After another 25 nautical miles in flight, the helicopter landed at the University of Virginia Medical Center by 11:52. As Robin Root wheeled Matt into the ER, knowing he had done his very best for this young man, he didn't hold out much hope that Matt would survive. He thought to himself, "It will take a miracle."

• • •

The Millers were maybe a mile from the Charlottesville airport, looking for some place quick to stop so they could get Michael something to eat. He had spent the night with swimming friends and promised his parents he would have eaten breakfast by the time they picked him up, and of course he had not. Time was short and even McDonald's would do. While Matt would never eat at McDonald's, which was far too unhealthy for him, Michael was a furnace, and a string bean, and would eat anything. Michael, sitting in the front passenger seat, took the call from Emily, and both Mike, who was driving, and Nancy, in the backseat of the rental car, could hear Emily's tears and hysterics through Michael's phone, though they couldn't make out what she was saying. They knew it wasn't good. Michael's face had turned pale. Emily actually could barely speak. She was just trying to get the words out to Michael between sobs. Michael summarized for his parents: Matt had been in a bad accident and they were flying him to the UVA hospital. Mike Miller pulled off the road into a strip mall parking lot. It was as if all the air had been sucked out from the rental car and they sat there for a moment, the three of them, in the strip mall parking lot, trying to catch their breath. This was where the narrative of their normal lives suddenly went off script, where the life they knew and loved and understood suddenly made no sense, became this fuzzy dream, this nightmare. Mike Miller just couldn't believe it. He was an attorney by training, a litigator, and he wanted more information.

He took the phone and spoke to Emily. What exactly had happened? How bad was it? Emily put Carrie on the phone, but she didn't know any more. Mike Miller told Carrie to call Rudy back, try and reach him and get more information. The Millers would drive straight to Matt's duplex, and pick up Emily, and they would go to the hospital together.

Mike Miller turned the car around, heading back into Charlottesville. They were all grateful, at least, that the call had come when it did, before their plane had taken off. Mike Miller had worked so hard his whole life, nobody worked harder, and he had built a wonderful life for himself and his family. He married his college sweetheart and paid his way through law school and clerked for a federal appeals judge and became a partner in a law firm and risked it all in an effort to save a struggling company and succeeded after a three-year slog and reaped the rewards and then came to Vanguard where he was so successful and so loyal and so beloved. The biggest thing in life for him to get upset about was UVA losing a football game it should have won. Until that moment. "Mike had this attitude that everything is going to be great in life," said one of his closest friends, Mike Missal, a former law partner. "Not that he's bulletproof, but good things seem to happen to him and his family. But all of a sudden there was a reality – that life isn't always going to be great. We're not invincible." At that moment, it was a huge challenge for Mike Miller to stay in control of his emotions, and he wasn't altogether winning. But he was fighting back his tears well enough to drive the car.

Nancy Miller was not crying. From that very first moment she held herself together. She was scared and she was upset, but she knew, not from some rational decision, but reflexively, driven by DNA or maternal makeup or her Gone-With-The-Wind roots or because she was a doctor's daughter, or maybe because of all of these things, that she must stay calm, that she would stay calm, and keep a clear head, and save her energy. Her son was going to need her. And letting her emotions run wild would only sap her strength. Her husband was ripped up, as he should be. Nancy was less emotional than Mike, or at least more in control of her emotions. Her father had been a surgeon in Roanoke. He would get these calls. She understood that horrible things can happen to anyone. Look at the families of soldiers in Afghanistan or Iraq. They lived in fear of these phone calls every day, and too often received them. Nancy Miller understood she was suddenly now being swept along on this rapidly moving stream, with no control of events, where all she could do was hope for the best. But that's what she was determined to do. Hope for the best and keep control of herself. Whatever was happening with Matthew Quinn Miller, and Quinn was her mother's maiden name, Nancy could help him and her family the most by staying calm.

Michael, tears welling in his eyes, was taking cues from his parents. He mostly sat quietly and prayed for his only sibling. Michael and Matt had been competitive as boys, warring over all the usual things, even who was better at ping pong. It really mattered who won at ping pong. But they were always close, and at college together had grown even closer. Michael was far from being a holy roller but he believed strongly in the power of prayer and it felt good to pray, or at least it provided him some comfort on that silent car ride back into town.

They swung by and picked up Emily, who hadn't been able to learn any more, and they hurried to the hospital. Mike Miller parked in the first space of the parking garage, ignoring the no parking sign. They saw the helicopter, the blades still turning, and Mike could see someone inside. He shook and pounded on the fence that surrounds the landing area, waved and shouted to get the man's attention. The man, the flight medic, came over. Mike asked if he had just transported Matt Miller. The medic wanted to know if Mike was the boy's father.

"He's my son," Mike said. "How is he?"

"Not good," the medic replied. "Critical."

Michael Miller described it as if his father had just taken a punch to the gut. He didn't topple over physically, but he did buckle emotionally. His father just repeated the word, in disbelief. *"Critical?"* Nancy's reaction was a little different. "Well, that's good," she told herself. "He's not dead. There's hope."

• • •

When the Millers entered the emergency room, and identified themselves as Matt Miller's parents, they were met by a chaplain. Mike Miller was rather insistent, and that's being kind. "We don't want to see a chaplain. We want to see a doctor!"

The family was taken to a little private waiting room, equipped with two couches, a chair, and phone. The hospital does this as a courtesy to families, so they can bear their grief in private, and have their own little base of operations for what is typically in these cases a long and horrible day.

Diane Hoffman, the social worker on duty, moonlighting on weekends to earn a little extra money for her children's college tuition, went to see them, to offer what support she could. Hoffman normally worked weekdays in one of the hospital clinics. The parents struck her as incredibly gracious, especially considering the circumstances, and very supportive of one another. They explained to her what Matt had been doing, how this had been such a fabulous family weekend until now. Emily was crying. Mike was pacing. Michael and Nancy just sat on the sofa. Nancy looked "physically like everything had been drained out of her," said Hoffman, "but there was also a sense of composure, 'I'm going to hold this together for as long as he needs me.'" Hoffman told the family the doctors would be in to see them as soon as they could, but right now they were examining Matt and doing their best to save his life. Mike Miller said he wanted to see his son, but she said they would need to wait for the doctors, who would be in to see them when they knew more. So the three Millers and Emily sat and worried and waited in this sterile little waiting room. They couldn't stand waiting but there was nothing else to do at this point but wait.

When AirCare 5 had taken off from Reeds Gap, Robin Root got on the radio and notified UVA that they were en route, and the hospital called a full trauma alert. A dozen people were beeped, and knew that in 15 minutes a critically ill patient would be arriving. The initial ER report, and countless subsequent medical records, would classify the accident as "bike versus car."

By 11:55 a.m., at most 80 minutes after impact, Matt Miller lay on the examination table in the primary trauma bay, room 61, in the Emergency Medical Department of one of the leading trauma centers in America.

A team of people was waiting for him around the table. There was a chart on the wall specifying where each person should stand – the primary trauma resident, the ER attending, the anesthesia resident, the nurse, the respiratory therapist and so on. These were people who had been trained especially for this moment, who lived for this moment.

Each wore a lead vest under his or her hospital gown because x-rays would be done right on that table. The first thing the team did was cut away Matt's clothing, so he lay there naked, under the very bright and warming lamps, and they surveyed him quite literally from the top of his head to the tip of his toes. From the neck down, aside from some scrapes and bruises, he looked relatively good. Then they ran through their own checklist in order of things that could kill him quickest, and it was alphabetical, ABCDE, airway, breathing, circulation, disability and exposure. His breathing tube – disconnected from the ventilator on the helicopter – had been reattached to the mechanical ventilation in the trauma bay, and staffers made sure his airway was secure and unobstructed. They listened to his breathing sounds to make sure they were equal in each lung and the chest didn't need to be drained of blood. They felt for pulses, checked his blood pressure, placed more IVs, and drew blood for tests. They checked his pupils for responsiveness (minimal, because of his sedatives and other drugs, but sufficient to show he was not brain dead). They tested his ability to move his limbs. They put a tube down his throat to suction out any blood and prevent vomiting. They put a catheter through his penis into his bladder to check for blood in the urine. They put a finger in his rectum and make sure it hadn't been perforated by a pelvic fracture. They looked in the ears for evidence of skull fracture, and found blood, a telltale sign. Their mantra was literally an eye on everything and a finger or a tube in every orifice. They x-rayed the chest and the pelvis for fractures. And of course they did a quick and immediate hands-on examination of his face to assess the extent of the injuries.

The doctor in charge in the trauma bay, by protocol, is the chief trauma resident. On this morning it was Daniel Kleiner, the chief resident responsible for trauma, who stood at the foot of the examination table, by Matt's feet, and conducted this world class symphony of trauma care. Kleiner and everyone else around the table had been told the basics – this was a UVA student injured in a bike versus car. Kleiner of course had no expectation that he should know the young man, whose face was so bashed up as to be unrecognizable. The face was also covered in blood, with breathing and suction tubes running into his mouth, and even the straps holding the suction tube in place were soaked with blood and red. Matt was still in the c-spine collar, hair all matted, and it just never occurred to Kleiner that he had met this young man several times.

A few times during this initial exam, the patient's name was read out, *Matthew Miller, Matthew Miller*, which sounded familiar to Kleiner, but he was too busy trying to save the patient's life to be thinking about the name. And then after ten minutes or so – the realization landed on him like an anvil. *This was the student following around Dr. Hanks.* Hanks was chief of general surgery and his path often crossed with Kleiner's, with Matt in tow. Kleiner's initial reaction to this realization was, "He's f– ed." Kleiner did not lack compassion. But he was a general surgery resident who had seen years of the grimmest traumas and he was just putting Matt in context, being honest about his own personal reaction.

After 14 minutes on the table, the initial survey was complete. The gold standard for such surveys at UVA is 13 minutes so this was pretty good. Matt was wrapped in warm blankets and wheeled to radiology just around the corner where CT scans were taken of his brain, spine, chest, and abdomen – just about everywhere – the first of many, many scans.

After seeing the first scan of Matt's brain, Dr. Kleiner, with a heavy but honest heart, thought to himself, this young man "is no longer going to be a medical student." Still, it was his job to find Matt's family and fill them in. Around 1:00 p.m. Dr. Kleiner met them in their little waiting area and told them doctors were still doing CT scans to assess the extent of Matt's injuries, and reviewing the results. He told them Matt may have serious brain injury but it would be premature at this point to say how extensive it was. He told the family he had recognized Matt, and had met him before, and that he was going to give John Hanks a call. He told the Millers and Emily that one can never predict with a head injury – it's wait-and-see. The family felt the doctor really didn't want to give them anything definite, that he was being vague, and they were right. Dr. Kleiner didn't feel it was appropriate to share his own harsh assessment at that point. Mike Miller is a man who cuts to the chase. He wasn't in a courtroom but he might as well have been because he asked the witness a simple and direct question that could not have been evaded: "Could our son die?"

"Yes."

. . .

Kleiner left the Millers and picked up the phone and called John Hanks, who even though it was early Sunday afternoon, was in his office at the hospital catching up on work. Kleiner told him, "There's a guy in here that you know. He's an undergraduate." Hanks was thinking to himself, "I don't know that many undergraduates and I can't imagine who it is."

Kleiner told him it was Matt Miller.

For many years, Hanks had taken part in a program run by the University in which undergraduates can sign up to shadow physicians around the hospital. But years ago, when he became chief of general surgery, he stopped participating in that program. He just didn't have the time on top of all his other responsibilities to let a student shadow him. He had found in his experience that most undergraduates shadowing doctors got bored very quickly and stopped coming after a time or two. Much of medicine can seem dull and monotonous, seeing patients in clinic, doing routine follow-ups. Sometimes Hanks found the students to be blatantly in pursuit of a letter of recommendation, and he would let them know politely but clearly that before that could happen, a lot would be expected, and then pretty quickly most of them would disappear as well.

In the fall of his second year, Matt Miller told his parents he was thinking about medical school. Matt liked people, liked science, and thought it would be a challenging and worthwhile life. He was 19 and didn't think about this at all in the context of his family history. His mother was the daughter of a doctor and granddaughter of a doctor and great granddaughter of a doctor. Her great-grandfather was George Washington Richards, known as G.W., a surgeon with the Confederate Army at Gettysburg. His medical bag, a wooden box, actually, made of Virginia walnut, and still filled with its original surgical instruments, including two saws, had been adorning for years – completely unbeknownst to Matt – the mantle in the home of Nancy Miller's younger sister in Jacksonville, Florida. It was Nancy Miller, after hearing about her son's interest in medicine, who suggested he might want to spend time with a physician at UVA. Nancy knew all too well that as worthwhile as being a doctor was, it wasn't like what one saw on television. When Matt checked into the shadowing program, he discovered he'd missed the deadline for that year. He called his father and asked for advice.

Mike Miller sat on the board of the Temple University Medical School in Philadelphia. Years earlier, the Temple medical school was on the verge of being decertified, and a new dean was hired to turn the place around, and he wanted an advisory board to help him. Raising money was going to be a critical part of that effort and this advisory board needed somebody with a financial background. One of the Millers' good friends through Little League in Wayne was a Temple physician, and that doctor suggested to the new dean, John Daly, that he recruit Mike Miller to the advisory board. And hearing Matt's dilemma, Mike Miller called John Daly, the Temple dean whom he'd come to know well, and asked if he had any ideas. Daly knew Hanks at UVA through their associations on national boards, and Daly called and asked Hanks a favor: Would he talk to this young man? Hanks, who had missed a few deadlines of his own in his day, agreed. He never imagined this second year student who showed up to observe him one day in clinic would come back again and again and essentially, as Hanks explained, "bond with everybody. Even the med students liked him. We sort of brought him in on the team, as the mascot."

Needless to say, John Hanks had grown quite fond of Matt. And only a few weeks earlier, he had met Mike and Nancy Miller for the first time, when they were in town for another football game. Matt and his parents had met for breakfast and Hanks was in the same restaurant, and Matt introduced them. Now he was about to meet them again, under the worst possible circumstances. He walked over to the emergency room, and greeted them in their waiting area. The Millers were immensely relieved to see him, to see somebody who was at least a little familiar, who knew their son. Mike in particular was growing pretty desperate. He wanted to see Matt. And Hanks agreed to take the four of them back to the trauma bay, two at a time.

If the father had not known this was his son, he would not have recognized him. "It was unbelievable a face could take that shape," Mike Miller said.

Again, Nancy Miller had a slightly different reaction. Matt had been such a handsome boy, model handsome in her eyes, with a sweet smile and All-American jaw. And as she looked at him on that gurney, she buried the heartache deep down. It would have to wait. There wasn't time for it, and certainly this wasn't the place for it. He looked awful. But he was alive. She told herself she must stay focused. The brain and the spine, these were the paramount issues. We need to find out about those.

Emily would be the first to tell you she wasn't thinking entirely rationally at the time. But her initial reaction was that Matt looked like himself, but asleep. His skin had no lacerations, and the face hadn't yet really begun to swell. His skull looked fine and she couldn't see any obvious place where his brain would have been damaged. She convinced herself he didn't look too bad. Hanks walked them back to their waiting area. "We have to let the doctors do their job," Hanks told the Millers. "At this point there's nothing we can do but pray."

• • •

Jason Sheehan, a neurosurgeon, was at home playing in the yard with his kids when he heard the news. There had been a trauma alert, and he was on call, so the resident on duty had phoned him, and Sheehan headed into the hospital. When Sheehan arrived, Matt was already getting his first scan of the brain.

The early CT scan showed several grave concerns. First, Matt had more than a dozen bruises, black and blue marks, hemorrhages, spread throughout all parts of his brain – the frontal lobes, temporal lobes, and the deeper structures known as internal capsules. The immediate concern was that these would swell. And swelling itself can be fatal, because the brain, encased in a very unforgiving skull, has nowhere to go. If the swelling can't be controlled quickly, the doctors must literally saw off the top of the skull, the cranium, giving the brain room to mushroom out the top. (This is what would later happen with Gabby Giffords, the Arizona congresswoman.) This procedure presents all sorts of dire risks and complications, and doctors hate to do it. They were fearful from the get-go that this was Matt's fate and it would be a very ominous sign. Then there was the issue of the bruises themselves. They could have damaged Matt's brain even before the swelling, causing permanent damage. It was so hard to know at that point if Matt had any cognitive function or how badly he was hurt.

Such broadly dispersed bruising also suggested another big risk to Matt's brain – what is known as diffuse axonal injury. All through the brain, Matt had little nerves, axons, which were encased in a covering for protection, like electrical wire inside a plastic or rubber coating. Upon impact with the car, from the blunt trauma, these axons got stretched. Pulled. The medical term is shearing. The question was whether the nerves themselves were stretched or sheared to the point of permanent injury, or whether only the casings were damaged, with the nerves inside remaining intact. Sheehan compared diffuse axonal injury to taking the nerves, or axons, and "putting them in a blender, shaking them up real fast and then expecting them to continue sending normal signals. That doesn't work very well."

J. Forrest Calland, the trauma surgeon who would assume overall responsibility for Matt's care, managing all the various specialists at work, gave two vivid if not entirely compatible analogies to help explain Matt's brain injuries. To understand the diffuse axonal injury, the stretched nerves, he said to imagine the peel of an orange getting twisted away from the pulp. As for how well Matt's brain could be expected to work after the degree of bruising and swelling it was experiencing, Calland compared that to "throwing your laptop out the second-story window."

Clearly, in Sheehan's judgment, controlling the swelling was the first and most important thing needed to be done to try and save Matt's life. And this was why it was so important, and so extremely fortunate, to get Matt into a world-class trauma center so quickly. Immediately, Sheehan was able to put Matt into a man-made, chemically-induced coma, to ease the work of his brain, to remove all the strain on it.

Literally, they could shut down the brain so it wouldn't think, wouldn't even tell the lungs to breath. Because having to think, having to work even on a subconscious level, would only tax the brain further, impede its healing, and exacerbate the swelling. The goal was to decrease the metabolism of Matt's brain, to give it a vacation from its duties so it could just rest and heal. Because of the body's own response, trying to rush blood and hormones to the damaged area to help with healing, "the swelling actually gets worse for the first few days rather than getting better," said Sheehan. "We knew if we were going to preserve his function and prevent any further injury, we had to keep the brain from swelling."

Ultimately, what doctors were concerned about was the pressure in Matt's brain. And the more the brain swelled, the higher the pressure inside his cranium would get. And it would be the high pressure, caused by the swelling, which could kill him.

The brain is the most carefully controlled and regulated organ in the body. There are many things happening in the healthy brain to make sure its blood flow and pressure changes vary little. If these fail-safes and controls are disabled – the result, say, of smashing one's face into a steel windshield post at 40 miles an hour – the brain very quickly loses its ability to control itself, and things go wildly, and fatally, out of whack. The brain will try to increase its blood supply – leading to more swelling and higher pressure – or cut back its blood supply, which can be equally fatal. In this induced coma, doctors tried to carefully regulate the flow of blood to Matt's brain, to keep the pressure at a level that wouldn't kill him.

A normal, healthy brain has an intra cranial pressure measured at five to ten millimeters of mercury. When Matt arrived in the hospital, the intra cranial pressure was already up over 15 millimeters of mercury. If that pressure reached or exceeded 20 for any sustained period, Matt would likely die, or suffer severe and permanent brain injury if he hadn't already. That was the challenge confronting doctors. Sheehan knew that swelling in the brain increases for up to three days after a trauma like this. The next 72 hours would be critical. That would be the first test. Could Matt hang on for three days? Could doctors contain the swelling, keep the pressure from soaring to fatal levels? Sheehan early that afternoon drilled a hole in Matt's head, through the skull and into the brain, and installed a pressure monitor, what is known as a Licox probe. The Licox measured pressure, temperature and oxygenation within the brain. With those measurements, doctors could monitor and regulate all three parameters in his brain.

As Sheehan looked down at Matt in the trauma bay, at his crushed face with the damaged brain behind it, and prepared to drill and insert the probe, he knew by this point that this was the college student who had been shadowing Dr. Hanks, that he was a UVA undergraduate hoping to go to medical school. Sheehan saw himself in this young man, for Sheehan had once been a University of Virginia undergraduate, and had held the same dream, and had seen it blossom into reality, going to UVA medical school, and now working as a neurosurgeon. Sheehan was going to do his very best for this young man, but at that moment he thought Matt had no chance of fulfilling that dream. After injuries this severe patients almost never recovered enough cognitive function to become doctors. He would do all he could do, but for a moment, to himself, he grieved for the future this boy had just lost.

• • •

Sheehan came out and explained the situation to the family, that the shaking of his brain, and the swelling, could be fatal, and that the next 72 hours would be critical. Matt's brain would continue to swell, but if they could contain that swelling, and if Matt got through that period, then he would likely survive. It was clear to all in that room that death was a very likely possibility.

Mike Miller decided at this point he needed to make some calls. He didn't know what to tell his parents, or how to tell them, so he put off calling them. He worried about his mother. She was so emotional, and to her family was everything. But after the first two calls, to people at Vanguard, he dialed his parents, who for many years now had been living in Roanoke, coincidentally not too far from where Nancy had grown up. They were in their early 80s now, and Mike's father had been successfully battling leukemia and lymphoma for a decade, but Mike had been putting off calling his parents because he didn't want to upset them, and he knew they'd want to come right up to Charlottesville, two hours to the north of Roanoke, and quite frankly that was the last thing he wanted. He had enough to handle. When the phone rang, Wanda, his mother, was sitting at the kitchen table in their two-bedroom home in a retirement community, Brandon Oaks, and her husband of 60 years, Sidney, was at St. Mark's Lutheran Church, where he spent so much of his time. Mike told his mother straight up – Wanda will never forget – "There's been an accident and Matt might die." Mike was trying with all his might to keep his own emotions in check, to upset his mother as little as possible. Mike Miller loves to tell stories, and conversations on the phone with his mother are rarely short, but this one was surprisingly short on both ends. What else was there to say? Mike made it clear that he did not want his parents to come now, and he would call again soon. As soon as she hung up, Wanda Miller picked the phone up again and called the church, trying to reach her husband, but there was no answer. He was probably out raking, or doing something in the garden. The man had been born and raised on a farm and had never lost his work ethic or his love and talent for making things grow. She tried to call one of her other sons, again no answer. She called her best friend in Roanoke, no answer again.

So she just sat at her kitchen table, beneath a Norman Rockwell painting on the kitchen wall, with her Bible and her Daily Word next to her, and just prayed: "God, you know, it's just you and me." She folded her hands and closed her eyes and fought back her tears and asked God to save her grandson, whom she had just seen the day before, with all his youthful energy and radiant smile. Wanda felt fear. *Matt can't die. What will we do without Matt?* Once you know a person, and love him, you can't imagine life without him.

The fourth call Mike made was to his administrative assistant, Nancy Ruffini. She had been his assistant since the day he came to Vanguard, in

1996, and he had called her at home countless times over the years. But when she answered the phone that Sunday afternoon and he said, "Nancy, this is Mike," she didn't know who it was. She couldn't recognize his voice, because it was so broken, so overwhelmed with emotion. He told her what had happened. This news could devastate any man, any father, she knew, but she frankly couldn't imagine Mike Miller ever getting over this. If that boy died, she instinctively knew right away, as much as Mike Miller loved Vanguard, he wouldn't ever be able to come back to work. He would just never recover. She knew how close he was to those boys. She answered the phone what seemed like every day when they called him at work. She knew how proud he was of both of them, how much he loved them, how he would juggle his incredibly busy schedule at Vanguard – he had 850 people working for him – so he could leave early and coach a little league team or slip out in the afternoons to watch a high school swim meet. Mike Miller was always on top of his game, always in control, a lawyer's lawyer who was always prepared, and here at this moment on this day he was lost. Nancy Ruffini spent hours just thinking about Mike and his son and the situation, and decided she needed to send an e-mail to the company's senior staff, which went out at 6:49 p.m.: "Mike called me this afternoon to tell me that Matt had been hit by a car while riding his bike. He is in the trauma center at the University of Virginia Hospital. He said Matt had a head on collision with the car. All the bones in his face are fractured and they are concerned about his brain. The next 72 hours are critical. Matt is definitely fighting for his life. Mike does not know when he will be back in the office. Please keep Matt and his family in your prayers. I will update you as I get more information."

• • •

Michael Miller, once he had a good idea of what had happened to his brother, and what Matt was facing, called his girlfriend back at Stanford, Linda Liu, whom he'd been dating since their second year of college at UVA. "He was trying to be really brave but his voice was shaking," Linda said. Then Michael called some swimming friends who were still in Charlottesville. One of them immediately called the coach, Mark Bernardino, and left him a message. Bernardino had spent the afternoon at a travel soccer game with his son, ironically, out in rural Nelson County, not too many miles from the scene of the accident, and only turned his cell phone back on as he neared his own home in Charlottesville. After listening to the message, Bernardino shared the news with his wife, Terry, and asked her what he should do. Terry had been a critical care nurse for many years, before their children were born, and was close friends with John Hanks, who had been at their wedding. She told her husband to buy food, lots of food, because they would not have eaten and will be starving only they won't know that they're starving because the last thing they will be thinking about is food. But bring them food. They will need food to maintain their strength. Go. Now. So he went to Jersey Mike's Subs and bought several large sandwiches and showed up. And he sat with them in the little room. He knew the family well, for he had coached Michael for four years, and Matt for one, and he had just stood with Michael on the football field the day before getting their championship rings. Bernardino was like family, and when he walked into that room, the Millers just felt lifted by his presence and support. Bernardino could see Mike was an emotional wreck, something he had not seen before but could surely understand. Mike told Mark Bernardino, "We might lose our son. Matt might not make it." Bernardino asked if he could see Matt, and Mike said no, Bernardino wouldn't want to see him, shouldn't see him. He wouldn't recognize him. Bernardino stayed positive. He told the family that Matt was one of the fittest people on the planet. If anyone could endure such an accident, Matt could.

Doctors were coming in now with news. Several CT scans showed that Matt suffered no spinal injury. Doctors said this could only be attributed to the fact that he was in such great physical shape. Then more good news. His heart and lungs, liver and kidneys, all seemed to be normal, tests confirmed. Bernardino said, "I like what I'm hearing!" Matt, it turned out, did have a broken right hand, and would need surgery for that. Nancy had been waiting all afternoon for news about the spine. She was tuned in to every nuance, every fact the doctors shared, braced herself for the worst, but so far she wasn't hearing anything from which there was clearly and absolutely no coming back. Matt would not be paralyzed. That was a positive.

• • •

After giving their statements to the National Park Service rangers, Mark and Mary Ann Harris were still quite shaken, but got back in their car and began the drive home. They stopped at the visitor center at Humpback Rocks, at milepost 5, because Mary Ann had to go to the bathroom. Her shirt was bloody, and she was nervous somebody would see her and wonder, but luckily, since the Parkway wasn't very busy, there was nobody around. Mark Harris wasn't even going to chance it. He was so covered in blood he stayed in the car. They continued on home, driving ever so slowly down highway 250 back into Charlottesville, just as the cyclists had planned to do. All afternoon and evening, Mary Ann, the former flower child who had become a social worker, couldn't help but think about that poor boy's mother in the hospital, possibly all alone. Mary Ann so badly wanted to go over to the hospital, to find the mother and tell her she'd been with her son on the mountain, and to comfort her now at this dreadful time. Mary Ann had this horrible vision of this poor mother in a sterile room watching this lovely boy die. But Mary Ann decided she couldn't go. The boy's mother would have no idea who she was, or what had happened on that mountain. She wouldn't want the comfort of a stranger. That night Mark Harris did call a former colleague at the UVA hospital and asked him to check on Matt's status and to keep him posted.

Ken Gregory waited around a couple of hours, gave his statement to the park rangers. One of the rangers told him, in so many words, that he didn't believe it was Ken's fault, but be prepared for whatever happens. This is America, the ranger told him. Lawyers get involved. You never know. Ken then somehow drove himself home. He doesn't really remember it. He was numb. The Porsche was still drivable, and he parked it in his garage. Ken was the lucky one. He walked away from the accident. Still, it had been the worst thing that ever happened to him.

National Park Service rangers closed the road, and several cars had stopped at the accident scene. Several drivers got out to find out what was happening, to offer help if they could. One southbound car had been pulling a bike trailer, and it turned out the driver was on his way to meet his wife and daughter, who had left much earlier in the morning and were riding their bikes down to Peaks of Otter Lodge. Husband, wife and daughter had been taking turns, two cycling and one driving, and this was his day to pull the trailer so they could ride. He felt a kinship and responsibility toward Rudy and Chris, being a cyclist himself. He offered to put their bikes on his trailer and give them a ride back to UVA. He'd catch up with his family later that night.

Rudy went home and immediately threw all his bloody clothes in the wash. Then Rudy walked up to Carrie's place. He felt this desperate need to talk with her and her roommates, to tell them what had happened. Carrie remembers him knocking at the door. He was standing in her doorway holding Matt's helmet, which was covered with blood. He was like a zombie, she said, like a ghost out of Shakespeare. She told him he could just throw the helmet away, but no, he insisted, he had to clean it for Matt, to keep it for him. Then he sat in her living room, with the brilliant afternoon sunlight streaming in as if nothing were wrong, and he wept uncontrollably as he told the story of what happened. He thought Matt was going to die. He thought by now Matt was already dead. After he left Carrie's, Rudy had no choice but to suck it up and go to his computer lab that evening and work on his group project. He never said a word to anyone.

Chris went home and decided that night he would never ride a road bike again. He listed his bike for sale on the internet. It was sold within a week.

• • •

John Hanks did one more thing for the Millers that afternoon besides provide them comfort. He called his colleague, Stephen Park, a facial plastic surgeon, whom he believed was the best surgeon at the University to rebuild Matt's face. Park, as it turned out, was leaving the next morning for the

Middle East, for a week of lectures and teaching. Hanks asked him to come in and operate on Matt.

Dr. Park was born in New York City, spent six years in Korea, moved back to America, to the Detroit suburbs, and attended Amherst College and the University of Michigan Medical School. He did his five year residency and training at Tufts in Boston, specializing in ear, nose and throat surgery. And within that specialty, he decided to become a facial plastic surgeon because it fit his personality. He is a meticulous man. He wants perfection and doesn't want to settle for less. And this kind of surgery, rebuilding faces after trauma, to make them look perfect and work perfectly – skin, muscles, nerves and bones – is where being meticulous and a perfectionist matters most and it really appealed to him.

He had three choices upon completing all his training on where to begin his practice. One choice was back in Boston, and he felt Boston was a great place to be young, to learn and be educated, but not the best place necessarily to be a practicing physician, and he wasn't keen on moving back. The next choice was the Mayo Clinic in Rochester, Minnesota, and the day he went for the interview, the wind chill was 30 below. His host at dinner said, "I guess this weather means you're not coming here," and Park insisted on going Dutch on the meal because he knew his wife wasn't moving to that climate and he didn't want to take the man's money. The final choice was Charlottesville. When he arrived at the airport, and the head of department picked him up, they were supposed to go to a formal restaurant that night. But his host said to him at the airport to "ditch the tie, no time for a fancy dinner, we're going to grab a burger at McDonald's because I've got courtside seats at the UVA-Florida State basketball game." Next morning, before a day full of meetings with all the big-shots, the head of the department picked him up and said first we've got a stop to make – with the golf pro at a local country club. "He knew how to push all my buttons," said Park. Nineteen years later, the rest was history.

Park came in and examined Matt and looked at the numerous CT scans of his face. In short, every bone in Matt's face was broken. The medical record describing Matt's myriad injuries was filled with incomprehensible medicalese, but there were some medical terms so vivid they needed no translation: "Central Facial Smash," "constellation of fractures," and "left orbital blowout." Matt's chin, jaw, cheeks, and bones around his eyes all shattered. At least 27 of his 32 teeth – damaged or destroyed.

Even though the force of the trauma was so extreme – face meets car at 40 miles per hour – the soft tissue on his face, the skin, didn't break, splatter or slash. Only the bones beneath. So if doctors could figure out a way to repair the bones, to rebuild the skeleton, the face had a chance of looking like a face. There were no guarantees that doctors could piece Humpty Dumpty back together, or whether the nerves in his face would ever work again, giving him the ability to smile or just stop from drooling. But while his face was swelling beyond recognition, the skin had only been stretched, not scarred. Park, by the way, found this to be simply miraculous, truly as if an Angel had been sitting on Matt's shoulder during the accident. He had never seen such a blunt trauma where the skin wasn't torn, ripped or lacerated. But at least Matt had that going for him and that was a start.

Ordinarily, rebuilding the face isn't an urgent priority. The face gets so much blood, unlike a lower leg or foot, there's little risk of immediate infection. In situations like Matt's – and believe it or not, there are all too often situations like Matt's – the face can wait a few days. There are two primary reasons to wait: One, why rebuild a face if the patient is going to die in a day or two from a brain injury? Usually it is best to wait and see if the brain injury resolves. Two, follow the Hippocratic Oath. Do no harm. Why submit the patient to even more invasion and suffering if he's going to die? Why compound his agony? The prudent thing, the standard procedure, was to wait. But Park was the best and he was leaving the country in the morning. The doctors conferred. Matt was critical but stable. They'd just have to wait and see on the brain. Calland, the trauma surgeon coordinating the care of all the specialists involved, gave the okay for them to do the facial reconstruction that night.

Park believed it was very likely, in a complicated and critical case like Matt's, that the chief resident on his service, Jared Christophel, who saw Matt when he arrived in the hospital, or the chief trauma resident, Kleiner, would have contacted him anyway, in the normal course of business, later that afternoon or evening and called him in to do the surgery. This would have happened regardless of the patient's background. Doctors get called in by other doctors all the time. And if the accident had happened a day later, and Park had already left for the Middle East, another surgeon would have stepped in, one of his very able colleagues. That's how the system is set up. Park did not see this as preferential treatment, but truly just another day at the office, albeit a very long one. Even though this surgery would leave him bleary-eyed for his flight to the Middle East in the morning, this was the life he had chosen.

Matt had been moved late that afternoon from the ER trauma bay up to the fifth floor Surgical Trauma ICU, and the Millers and Emily had found a new little waiting room up there in which to camp out. They were told Matt was about to undergo lengthy and extensive surgery to rebuild his face. They didn't know much more than that. But they were looking for any sign, any reason to be positive. And they determined this must be a good thing. They reasoned to themselves, this must mean doctors think Matt's going to survive. It really meant no such thing. It was just a hedged bet, considering the circumstances.

Park assembled his team, primarily assisted by Jared Christophel, the chief resident in his department.

To rebuild a face, the surgeons follow simple principles, elementary concepts. First, you try to begin with what is still fixed and solid and intact, and attach whatever loose parts you can to the fixed parts. If you start by attaching loose pieces together, one to another, there is no guarantee they will ever connect to the fixed parts, or line up to look like a face. In the computer files of these surgeons are photo after photo of patients with injuries less severe than Matt's whose reconstructed faces look backed in, or dented, or with eyes way too far apart, or noses flat like an iron. How well the skin and soft tissue lay on top of the bones, how much a face is shaped like a face, depends on the reconstructed frame below. The second rule to follow is that you try to start with teeth, to line them up if they are intact, because that way there's a good chance the rest of the facial bones will follow suit. But of course Matt had only a few teeth that could serve as a road map.

The surgeons used titanium plates and self-tapping screws to reconstruct the skeleton. Imagine an erecter set. They used hand tools, high-tech pliers, to bend the titanium plates to form the shapes they wanted. In the most elementary sense, Park and his team were carpenters, architects and engineers all rolled into one. Where there were only bone fragments, not substantial enough to hold a screw, surgeons hoped these would coalesce and heal around a plate. The surgeons worked for hours, and in the end, finishing well after midnight, needed 7 plates and 32 screws. They wired his jaw shut, so Matt's new titanium face wouldn't shift or fall out of alignment as the bones healed.

Around 1:00 a.m., Park went to find the family in a small waiting room up by the fifth floor ICU. Mike, Michael and Emily were dozing in chairs. Nancy was actually asleep on the floor, her head resting on her coat, and Park bumped her head when he opened the door. He told them that this was one of the worst cases he'd ever seen. "Your son's face was like a piece of fine china dropped from 20 feet," he told them. He was incredibly proud of his crew, and felt the team had done its absolute best. He recounted for them the surgery, step by step, and regarding all the little pieces of shattered bone just floating around, too small to reattach, he said, "You can't fix those bones. You just hold it all together and hope they'll heal."

The family did find one reason to smile. Several times during the surgery, Park said, Matt's pulse was so low it triggered alarms. The heart monitor was set to go off at 50. "It only took a moment to see that he was fine," Park said, "that he was some kind of athlete."

Park also told the Millers that two things saved Matt's life: "his helmet and his face."

"What do you mean his face?" Mike Miller asked.

The face has a "number of air pockets," Park explained, "and nobody really knows what they're doing there. Are they to lighten the skull, to help our voices resonate, or to act as an air bag? When you get a blow, that force is transmitted into the air pocket rather than to what is directly behind it, which is the brain."

"He may have been saved by the severity of his facial fractures," Park said.

So Matt's face had served as a crumple zone. Amazing what one learns in the middle of the night.

Around 2:00 a.m., the Millers finally left the hospital. Before going to their hotel, the Marriott Courtyard, right across from the hospital, they were directed by Emily to her dorm, where they dropped her off. On what was also the worst day of her life, Emily fell asleep clutching a teddy bear Matt had given her on their first Valentine's Day, when both were high school seniors. Climbing into bed, Emily pushed a button on the bear, which recited a recorded message in Matt's voice: "I'm Emily's and she's mine."

Sometime between 3:00 and 4:00 a.m., just as the Millers were drifting off to sleep, Nancy Miller's cell phone rang, and all three bolted upright in bed with a cold wave of dread and adrenalin. Nancy had given her cell phone as the primary contact number, and who else would be calling at this hour? It had to be the hospital. The news had to be bad. Mike, who can be emotional but deals with life straight on, picked up the phone and answered. It indeed was the hospital calling. People in billing needed more information about Matt's insurance. Mike calmly said he'd call back with the information in the morning.

———

CHAPTER FOUR

When Emily awoke, she rushed right back over to the hospital, so relieved and overjoyed to learn Matt was still alive. She was completely irrational, and didn't really understand his injury, thinking, "Well, if he lived through the first night, that means he'll live through the second and the third." It didn't mean that at all.

The brain injury could be getting worse, and death could come at any moment, caused by any number of complications, of which swelling was only one. But Emily didn't understand this. She had repeatedly asked doctors the day before to enumerate the worst case scenarios, but they had not. They had been vague, with lots of "we don't know" and "we'll have to wait and see." There were many terrible things that could still turn fatal. But Emily in her naïveté locked on to only this: Matt lived through one night, why can't he live through them all?

She was overjoyed to find him alive, but this was tempered by her reaction when she actually approached his bedside. When she had seen Matt on Sunday, for the first time after the accident, she thought he looked like himself, only asleep. But by Monday morning, with the swelling of the accident compounded by more swelling from six hours of facial surgery, Matt was like one of those candy M&M characters on the television commercials, a stick figure with a giant colored head, and in his case his face was a blend of black, blue and yellow.

While there could never be a good time for such a horrible accident, what was happening now with Matt couldn't have come at a worse time for Emily.

First of all, and worst of all, her parents had separated and were headed for divorce. Emily was the oldest child, and was dealing with this from a distance, and that was so difficult. The dissolving of her parents' marriage was a slow, gradual, painful process. They had just drifted apart. This is never easy to deal with for anyone, ever. Secondly, there had been so many other bad things happening in her life. Emily's maternal grandfather had just died, and so had her mother's sister, and an uncle on her mom's side, all in the last several months. And when she learned of Matt's accident, on top of all these other deaths and difficulties in her personal life, she just felt like, *Really? Now what? What more can happen and when will it stop?* On top of all that, she had just transferred to Virginia. She had been there just over two months. She lived in a drab, remote dorm, Gooch, for transfer students, "in a tiny closet of a room." She was just getting adjusted, still incredibly nervous whether she could cut it there academically. She was in the same physics class with Matt, for pre-med majors, because Emily, whose mother was a doctor, was also thinking about medical school. She had been studying physics in her tiny room when Carrie Barnes, one of her few good friends at school besides Matt, had called with the news about Matt.

Emily was always smart enough, or always thought she was pretty smart, but she never really cared in high school. It's not that she didn't care, but she didn't care enough to bear down. She took the hardest classes, and hung out with the smartest kids, but her grades were Bs, nothing special, certainly not at Radnor High School. Maybe her parents just assumed she was trying hard, doing her best, and that she would do well because they were both pretty accomplished and successful people, but they didn't ever stay on top of her, ask to check her homework, fuss over her grades, and so her grades reflected her indifference to them. Her parents might have tried talking to her a few times but she didn't listen. She just sort of drifted through high school, without much focus. She always figured she'd go to college but unlike almost every other kid at Radnor she didn't obsess over it or take SAT prep classes or hire consultants or apply to a dozen schools. She applied to two – The University of North Carolina and East Carolina University, and she got in only at ECU. Emily had grown up in Chapel Hill, where her mother had gone to medical school, but she had also lived in Greenville, home of ECU, when her mother did a year of residency there. Emily only transferred into the Radnor Middle School in 7th grade, just a year before Matt asked her to the 8th grade formal. Her dad had taken a job in the Philadelphia area and moved the family there, and that's one of the things she and Matt had in common. Most of the kids in Radnor had lived there their whole lives. Matt moved into the Radnor school district when he was in third grade, when his dad took the job at Vanguard. Matt was a big jock, great at baseball, swimming and golf, and through sports it was easy for him to make friends. Emily was shy by nature, and not outgoing, so making friends was harder for her.

This was one of the great things about her relationship with Matt. He was not only so confident in himself, and often so successful at whatever he applied himself to, but he was so confident in *her*, and always so supportive and encouraging of her to try things, go for things. She might have found her way and her focus on her own, who knows, that is a part of growing up and becoming mature. But Matt's confidence in her so buoyed her own confidence. For instance, at East Carolina, she finally found her motivation and discipline as a student and rocked every course, and she knew after two years there she was going to transfer, and she got into lots of great universities. She decided on Virginia not only because of Matt – after all, they'd survived two years of a long-distance relationship already, and could no doubt survive two more – but because of all the many reasons everyone loved UVA. It was a fabulous school in a fabulous place.

Emily knew she was emotional and a weepy mess that Sunday and Monday and made no apology for it. She loved Matt. And she had never been one to hide her emotions, never able or willing to conceal if she were angry or upset or even just having a bad day. She never felt that crying was a sign of emotional immaturity. It was just how she expressed her fear and grief. She was not a person who could plaster on a happy face. With Emily what you saw was how she felt.

And now, seeing Matt in the ICU bed that Monday morning, what struck her most, even more than his obvious and extensive injuries, was his vulnerability. Matt had always been so in control, so confident about his success at anything he put his mind to. His hunger to try new things and master them was so much a part of how he defined himself. And here he lay in this bed, in a coma, a machine breathing for him, a catheter collecting his urine, so many medicines keeping him alive. *He was just laying there,* she thought, *saliva all over himself. He seemed like a baby, so vulnerable.* She knew how much he would hate being like this, and knowing that, on top of everything else, made her so inconsolably sad.

• • •

Matt continued to get CT scans of his brain – at 1:43 a.m., right after his facial surgery; again at 10:02 a.m. Sheehan compared those two scans that Monday morning and did not see "any appreciable change." Matt's cranial pressure was still dangerously high, but not yet to the point where they'd need to surgically remove the top of his head. Because of their careful regulation and close attention, horrible had not gotten more horrible. That was a good thing.

Doctors would bring Matt out of his induced coma every few hours to check his responsiveness, and the first time they lightened his sedation, Matt tried to pull out his breathing and feeding tubes. Such behavior is a good signal of brain activity, but not good for a patient's immediate well-being. Staff put mitts on Matt's hands and restrained his arms by his side.

The ICU staff let Mike, Nancy, Michael and Emily visit Matt in his room in pairs. The family talked to him but didn't know what, if anything, he understood. When doctors lightened the sedatives, sometimes Matt would open his eyes when they spoke, but sometimes not. "Squeeze my finger," his mother would say. Sometimes he would. Other times not.

Nancy Miller so desperately wanted to do something for her son. She wanted to help him, save him. It was so hard for her to sit there and be passive and wait, to leave his fate so entirely in the hands of God and doctors. She had given birth to him, nursed him, taught him to read and to ride a bike, to tie his shoes and to swim and even to bake muffins. She had tucked him in a thousand nights, but what could she do for him now? Well, she could do one thing. In fact, she fixated on it. Matt wore contact lenses. And in the emergency room on Sunday, nurses examined both eyes carefully, found the contact in his right eye, and removed it, but found no contact in his left eye. They just assumed the impact of the collision had dislodged it, and that it was probably lying somewhere on the Blue Ridge Parkway. For some reason, perhaps a mother's instinct, Nancy Miller couldn't accept this. She was the one who first told the nurses about the contact lenses, and when they couldn't find the second lens the first time, she asked them to look again Sunday afternoon. No lens.

On Monday, with new nurses on duty, she tried again. She asked a nurse Monday morning to look in his eye, a third time now. There was no contact lens. She still, believe it or not, wasn't satisfied. Michael was thinking, come on, Mom, give it a rest. Emily was thinking why does she obsess so much over this stupid contact lens that isn't there? But what if it were there? It could cause an infection, or scratch his cornea. Matthew Quinn Miller might die or never be himself again, and there was nothing she could do about that, but Nancy wasn't going to allow her son to have a scratched cornea if she could help it. Well, in the afternoon Monday another nurse came in to Matt's ICU room and Nancy Miller asked her to look in Matt's eye for a fourth time. And wouldn't you know it, on the fourth try, this nurse found the contact lens in his eye, and took it out.

• • •

The first guy you call when you think your son might die is not your boss, but your best friend. In Mike Miller's case, Jack Brennan happened to be both. Brennan, the chairman and former chief executive officer of Vanguard, the man who hired Mike Miller in 1996, was sitting on his bed Sunday afternoon, getting dressed for a dinner in New York, when he received the first phone call Mike had made after Matt's accident. Mike called many people that Sunday afternoon and evening, because calling friends and family was one powerful way in which he coped. But Jack Brennan was the first call. Mike considered it the greatest day of his professional life when Jack Brennan took a chance on him and hired him to help him run Vanguard. Brennan wasn't always the easiest guy to get to know but they hit it off from the very first phone call, and in the ensuing 12 years they had become far more than colleagues. Brennan considered Mike the most loyal man he'd ever known, both professionally and personally. Jack was supposed to fly out Monday afternoon to Australia, for a week of meetings and talks, but he wasn't about to be in the air or 15,000 miles away if Matt Miller died. He had to go down to Capitol Hill Monday morning – a meeting he couldn't miss – and after that he just rented a car and drove down to Charlottesville, unannounced, uninvited and unexpected, to offer his support and assistance to his friend.

Mike Miller had been dire on the phone, and Jack Brennan was just hoping that when he arrived Matt would still be alive. When Jack walked into the intensive care waiting room on the fifth floor, the two men bear-hugged. Mike teared-up. Jack Brennan is not a crier but he was fighting like hell not to cry at that moment. It meant the world to Mike that Jack had shown up to offer his support. Jack's first question was, "What can I do to help?"

Even when you run a mutual fund company with $1.5 trillion in global assets, there is a limit to your influence. There really was nothing Brennan could do, other than offer his own prayers and sit with his friend and comfort him. He did offer to swing by the Millers' home in Wayne and pick up the mail, or water the plants, whatever Mike and Nancy needed. Just across the hall from the intensive care unit, incredibly, was an outdoor terrace. What a blessing this was to families. The weather was still sunny and warm for early November, and Jack Brennan, the Millers and Emily sat on benches and talked, next to planters, on a sunny, dry afternoon, a remarkably peaceful and serene setting. They could see other people down below, outside on the streets and sidewalks, going about their normal lives. This was actually a comfort. It almost seemed surreal to be in such a pleasant space with Matt fighting for his life not much more than 30 feet away.

The Millers told Brennan everything that had happened so far, how the surgery had gone the previous evening and how they were now in a holding pattern, wait and see. Because of the e-mail by Mike's administrative assistant, Nancy Ruffini, to the senior staff, which had circulated throughout

Vanguard, Mike was getting dozens of e-mails and calls, and he told Brennan to please thank everyone for their prayers and to tell them he was sorry he hadn't responded. Brennan found this to be so Mike. Mike Miller was one of the world's greatest thank-you guys, known throughout the company for thanking his people when they had done a great job. Jack had always preached and truly Mike understood that it wasn't the executives that made a company great, but the rank and file, the people who actually did the research and spoke with the investors and put the vision and philosophy into practice. It was so like Mike in the middle of a personal crisis still to be thinking about others, to be feeling badly he hadn't thanked them. Brennan that afternoon was careful not to stay too long, maybe an hour. Mike rode the elevator down with him to the main lobby and walked him out. Here Mike stopped and got very emotional. "I don't know what to do," Mike said. "What if he dies?" Jack knew that Mike was many things, but deep down and to his core he was a litigator, and litigators are always in control. But not Mike Miller, not now. Brennan believed Mike was trying his best to be strong and composed around his family, and Jack was grateful that he could be a friend, give Mike a chance to express his fears and doubts.

That evening, Brennan sent an e-mail to the senior staff, updating them on his visit, telling them he felt better about the situation than he had the day before, but "no matter what happens from here, Matt has a long road ahead under the best of circumstances." Brennan also wrote, "This won't surprise you: Mike feels badly that he hasn't responded to the many notes of concern and support that he's received all day." Brennan knew this piece of information would comfort his colleagues. They would see the good part of Mike was still working, that he wasn't completely lost in grief, and he was still thinking like the Mike they knew. And true to form, Mike Miller sent an e-mail to Jack the next morning: "Nancy, Michael and I can't thank you enough for coming down yesterday. You are an unbelievable friend. There is no one who I hold in higher esteem, and no one whose presence could have meant more to me yesterday."

• • •

Monday was pretty much a blur. Bernardino, the swim coach, stopped by again, as did Hanks. Other members of the swim team came by, dropping off food, pretty soon mountains of food. Seeing all these swimmers was especially uplifting for Michael, who had been captain the previous year, and found great comfort in the repeated embraces of his swimming family. Matt McLean, a big, strong, tall, Adonis-like swimmer, squeezed Michael in probably the tightest and most emotional hug of his life. When a guy can win an NCAA championship in the 500 yard freestyle, which Matt McLean would later do, he's got some seriously powerful arms to wrap you tight. Michael also visited the hospital chapel a few times. At that point that's really all you have, family and community support, and prayer.

The four of them, Mike, Nancy, Michael and Emily, continued to visit Matt, in shifts, two on and two off, and held his unbroken left hand and talked to him. Sheehan, the neurosurgeon, told them that he believed this would help Matt. "I've long felt that familiar faces and voices, mainly in Matt's case, voices, do have some bearing on the outcome," Sheehan explained. "When his parents are in the room speaking, I'm pretty confident that that plays a role in someone's recovery, even when they're in a pharmacologically-sedated status. The brain is not completely shut off. It keeps one's emotional state intact, and that really helps. If you don't have some degree of hope and love and compassion and support, I'm not sure that one's perspective in a situation like that is quite as good, and it truly will have an impact on the outcome." He had no data to support this, just his own experience and instinct.

There was very little change in Matt's status as Monday rolled into Tuesday. The swelling of the brain was continuing, but modestly. On Tuesday at 3:33 a.m. another scan: Hemorrhages and contusions "do not appear to be significantly increased in size," the test result stated, though the swelling "may be slightly more prominent."

Every hour that Matt hung on, and didn't get worse, moved him an hour closer to survival. But the passage of time felt like an eternity. Emily felt that maybe in a crazy way because she was so upset this had forced the Millers to remain calm. In addition to drawing comfort from the community of swimmers, Michael talked often with his girlfriend, Linda, who was enrolled with him at Stanford now working on a PhD in biomedical informatics. Mike Miller was on the phone or e-mailing with his parents, brothers, friends and colleagues, updating them two, three or four times a day, and trying to get every update he could from every doctor or nurse. Mike wanted answers and if he couldn't get answers he at least wanted information, and then he wanted to share it. Nancy tried her best to stay focused, sharp, to ask all the varied specialists all the right questions. She drew great comfort talking to her sister Gail in Jacksonville, the last person in the world who still called her Nancy Jane, which was how Nancy was known in the family growing up. But even on the phone with Gail, Nancy was always measured, controlled, positive but realistic. This was exactly how Gail expected Nancy Jane to be and how Gail imagined she would have been herself. This was how Daddy had raised them.

In a way, for Emily, the Millers became surrogate parents. They made sure she was eating, and got home safely at night, and expressed concern about her missing classes. They were so together and positive and hopeful that this gave Emily great comfort and kept her tethered to her own sanity. She cried so much as it was. Where would she have been without their support and companionship? She realized that she was just the girlfriend, and she asked repeatedly in those first couple days, "Do you all need to be alone?" "Should I leave?" She tried to be deferential, but they were insistent and inclusive from the very start. You belong here. After a doctor would share with them the latest test result, or explain what they might be doing next, Emily would play an active and incisive role in the family discussion. Emily even in her emotional state wanted all the facts, the truth, just like the Millers. She had begun to feel that not all the doctors were forthcoming with the truth. She felt they should be more transparent. She told herself that if she were ever to become a doctor at the bedside of a critically ill patient she would always remember what it was like for her as the loved one, the girlfriend, desperate to get whatever information she could. And if a family asked her a question, she would respect them with the truth.

On Tuesday, and into Tuesday night, the Millers were joined in the Surgical Trauma ICU waiting room by two African American parents. Their son, a third year engineering student, had been driving home to Petersburg,

Virginia, to vote in the Presidential election when he was involved in a car accident. After Michael heard their story he thought to himself: *This is Election Day! Of course!* Michael had been passionately interested in the Presidential race. He had worked the previous summer for Philadelphia Mayor Michael Nutter, and was the most interested in politics and public policy of anyone in the family, and was thinking about a career in public service law. From the moment of Matt's accident, that had all seemed so unimportant. He had cared so deeply, but now he had completely forgotten. The outside world was a million miles away. These other parents, who shared the Millers' fruit baskets and gift baskets, watched the election results on the television in the waiting room that evening. Michael was struck by how much this meant to them. Even with their son in the ICU, they were moved to tears seeing Barack Obama elected as the first African American President of the United States. Being in the waiting room with them, Michael felt in a small way part of this historic night. He was glad to see these parents had something else to think about besides their own son, whose injuries, thankfully, were not as severe as Matt's.

• • •

On Wednesday afternoon, Rudy finally mustered the resolve to go visit Matt. He hadn't said a word about the accident to anyone, other than Carrie on Sunday afternoon. He'd been forcing himself to study, to get through this now truly hellish week, but he hadn't been sleeping. He'd wake up with nightmares, hardly a surprise. Chris was suffering the same way. He'd be sitting in class and a flashback would hit him like a lightning bolt, sending a shudder right through him. Rudy wasn't allowed into the ICU room so he couldn't actually see Matt. In the waiting area, Rudy spoke with the family briefly, and mentioned in passing Dr. Harris. Both Nancy and Mike had heard comments from nurses about "the doctor on the mountain" who'd been calling to check on Matt's condition. But the Millers didn't know anything about him nor did they comprehend why he'd be calling. After Rudy said Dr. Harris's name a couple more times, Mike Miller stopped him. He'd been hearing lots of doctors' names all week now, and meeting lots of doctors in person, but who was Dr. Harris? "He's the doctor on the Parkway who saved Matt's life," Rudy told him. This was news to the family. They hadn't heard any of this. Rudy's details were thin, just that Dr. Harris, whoever he was, happened to be there and cared for Matt until the ambulance came. Mike Miller was puzzled. He'd have to find out more.

• • •

Tim Buckley, the Vanguard executive who introduced Matt to triathlons, who helped him buy Black Beauty, literally felt an intense heat, a burn sweep through his body as he stood by the front door, in the foyer of his home, on Sunday evening when Mike Miller called him, and told him, "They don't know if he's going to make it. They told me he may not make it."

A father should never have to speak those words about a child, Buckley felt, especially a father with as much love for his son as Mike had for Matt. Buckley had young children of his own, and he had worked closely with Mike long enough to appreciate what a great relationship Mike had built with his boys, a warmth and familiarity that he hoped to achieve with his own children as they grew older. The news hit hard. Buckley just felt so bad for Mike, and obviously for Matt, whom he had come to know. But truth be told, he also felt a horrible guilt. "We had encouraged Matt to get into this sport," Buckley said. "I pointed him to this bike. The bike he was riding had my equipment on it. You go through your mind, *What if the tires failed? What if the wheels failed – the wheels I gave him?*"

An hour after Mike's call Sunday, Buckley sent Mike an e-mail at 8:15 p.m.: "I am sick about Matt's injuries. I am encouraged because he is as strong as an ox and he is surrounded by love. I will continue to pray for him. He is a special guy and friend."

Not far from Buckley, in Newtown Square, Pennsylvania, Chris McIsaac was also getting the news, and feeling the same sorrow, helplessness, and, in truth, responsibility for what happened. McIsaac was 34, and probably of all the riders that summer at Vanguard had become the closest with Matt, and stayed in regular contact with him via e-mail and phone all fall. Matt loved to tell McIsaac about his workouts, and often had technical questions about derailleurs or training techniques for him and Buckley. "We certainly had a role in fanning the flames," McIsaac said. "I know intellectually that we were not responsible for this. This type of stuff just happens, and I think it's just chance more than anything else. Nevertheless, there's this gnawing feeling that you had something to do with it. That was a pretty awful feeling, knowing that you had been a big part of his love affair with cycling."

Bill McNabb, Vanguard's new CEO, had only replaced Jack Brennan the previous August, being promoted from one of a few managing directors, like Mike Miller, to running the company. McNabb didn't feel the same guilt or sense of responsibility as Buckley and McIsaac, but he shared their affection for Matt, and he was much closer to Mike Miller than either of the other two. He had worked side by side with Mike since Mike had arrived at Vanguard. He considered him a close friend. Only a few months earlier, the day Jack Brennan announced he was retiring as chief executive, "the first thing Mike did was he came bursting into my office," McNabb recalled. Mike then shut the door and told McNabb, "Jack told me not to come up and see you and we're trying to keep this top secret and there's a line out your door but I'm ignoring them." Mike Miller of course knew that McNabb would be named the new CEO. Then, according to McNabb, Mike congratulated him and basically offered to quit. "Jack hired me, Jack put me in this place, Jack gave me all this and I could totally understand if you want to go in a different direction," Mike told McNabb. McNabb looked at his friend in shock and disbelief. "Are you kidding me?" McNabb said. "I love you and I love what you do." McNabb later explained, "That's Mike. He has an incredible sense of loyalty and that's what makes him so special."

When McNabb heard the news on Sunday afternoon, he was actually at home writing his retirement speech – an exercise for a two-day program at Harvard for newly-minted CEOs, what McNabb said was affectionately known as CEO Kindergarten. Brennan had encouraged McNabb to continue with the program Monday and Tuesday as scheduled, which McNabb did, but he was prepared to leave at any moment, should, frankly, Matt die.

McNabb doesn't remember a thing about those two days at Harvard, or how he finished writing or delivering his faux retirement speech.

But he does remember talking with Buckley and McIsaac and the three of them deciding they just had to go to Charlottesville on Wednesday to see Matt and Mike. They chartered a small plane from the local West Chester, Pennsylvania airport – not the usual Vanguard way, but there just wasn't time to go commercial – and flew down Wednesday afternoon. "We didn't really know what we were doing," McNabb said, "just going to go and try to be there."

Mike Miller had frankly discouraged everybody from coming. He had even told his brother Dennis, with whom he is extremely close, and his close friend and former law partner Mike Missal, and his parents and virtually everyone else from out of town not to come. He had enough on his hands. The locals had been pouring in – Hanks, Bernardino, swim team families, students – but they would only stay a short while and leave.

Again, unannounced, McNabb, Buckley and McIsaac showed up at the fifth floor ICU on Wednesday afternoon. They sat on that same outdoor terrace, and made small talk with Mike, Nancy, Michael and Emily, just as Jack Brennan had done, for about an hour. The only difference was that on the way to the hospital they had stopped to buy a case of Diet Cokes for Mike because everyone knew he loved Diet Cokes and they couldn't think of anything else to bring. "He looked exhausted," said McIsaac. Mike gave them a matter-of-fact accounting of what had happened since Sunday. Even though the sedatives had been lightened, and Matt was no longer in a medically-induced coma, he was still largely unresponsive, and the 72-hour waiting period had pretty much expired.

Mike, always gracious, even in his grief, got up to walk the three men to the elevator. He was thanking them for coming and telling them that the doctors kept repeating that it was good for Matt to hear familiar voices. As they entered the elevator, Buckley said, "Well, make sure you tell Matt we were here and that we're praying for him." And at that point, in the privacy of the elevator, as if conspiring, Mike Miller said to the three men, "Well, do you want to see Matt? I thought you guys didn't want to see Matt because he looked so bad?"

"No, we'd love to see him," said Buckley. "But we didn't want to ask. We didn't want to be pushy."

They were in the first floor lobby now.

"Well do you think you can handle it?" Mike asked them.

All three assured him they could.

Only relatives were allowed in the ICU, and so far, only Mike, Nancy, Michael and Emily, along with Dr. Hanks, had been in the room to see Matt. Mike Miller was a scrupulous, meticulous man. He believed in following rules. But not this time. He felt that the potential benefit to Matt – hearing the familiar voices of these three men – was worth breaking hospital rules.

"Just follow me and don't stop," he told them.

They rode the elevator back up, walked through the foreboding doors into the ICU, and right into Matt's room.

All three visitors from Vanguard were incredibly anxious, not so much about breaking the rules, but preparing themselves for what they were about to see.

"He looked like a stretched balloon," Buckley recalled. "There were no facial features, but you knew it was Matt."

"He almost looked like a watermelon from the forehead down," said McIsaac. "Big and puffy. You couldn't make out any features of his face."

They gathered around his bed. McIsaac and Buckley on one side. Mike and McNabb on the other.

Mike Miller said to his son, "Matt, some friends are here to see you: Bill McNabb and Tim and Chris."

Matt's eyes opened and stayed open.

He reached up, as if trying to give them a hug. But his arms were restrained.

Did he recognize them? It seemed that way.

Not knowing what else to do, the men started talking, making small talk at first, but that soon turned to trash talk.

McIsaac told Matt that his pulse during surgery – 42 – was lower than Buckley's had been during a recent knee surgery.

Matt gave a thumbs-up.

Then Buckley said, "Hey, Matt, McIsaac is burning up that the last ride you went on together you dropped him. He thinks he can take you when you get out."

Matt, passionately, shook his head, as if to say, "No way."

At that point, Mike Miller simply wept. It was shockingly, abundantly, clear to all four of them that Matt understood the conversation and was responding. He was alert. He was coherent.

As incredible as this moment had been, it was just a moment. Matt's eyes quickly closed as if from immense fatigue. Mike Miller kissed his son on the forehead and the four men left the room and the ICU and stopped in the lobby to confirm with one another that what they had just seen had really happened.

All four men knew they had just witnessed a moment they would remember all their lives.

"I don't think I felt any gravity for a while," McNabb said. "I sort of floated down the hall."

• • •

Within hours, doctors had come to the same conclusion. They felt Matt would survive. He had endured the 72 hours. The swelling of his brain had peaked and was even now finally beginning to recede, and when they lightened the sedatives, Matt showed flickers of cognition. Deep down, below that balloon-like face, beyond the fog of narcotics and sedatives, inside that bruised brain, Matt's mind was still working. To some degree Matt was still Matt. Dr. Hanks, who had been visiting every day, had to a large degree become the synthesizer, the person who ferreted out medical information from the many specialists and distilled it for the Miller family. He found them about 7:00 Wednesday evening, gathered them together in the family waiting room outside the ICU, and told them, "It's time for hugs and kisses. Matt's going to make it."

Everyone did hug and kiss, and they felt a huge weight had been lifted.

Mike, not surprisingly, was the most visibly buoyant. After hours of rejoicing and sharing the good news by phone with friends and family, he decided this was the perfect moment to call this Dr. Harris, to find out more about what had happened on that mountain. And if this doctor had indeed saved his son's life, as Rudy said he had, than this mysterious Dr. Harris deserved to know that physicians felt now on this night with confidence that Matt Miller was going to survive.

Mike doesn't know how he got the number or what time it was when he called Dr. Harris. It could have been 2:00 a.m. Mike was flying so high he didn't know or care. It was actually around 10:00 p.m. when Mark Harris answered his home phone.

They talked for half an hour or so. Mike told Mark Harris about the extent of Matt's injuries, about how he had just survived the crucial 72-hour test. Mark Harris told Mike Miller his story from the Parkway. Mike was breaking down in tears. Mark Harris was breaking down in tears.

"When your son drove away in that ambulance," Mark Harris told Mike, "I turned to Mary Ann and said to her `that boy won't make it to the hospital.'"

Both men, truly, were just giddy. Mark Harris never expected Matt to live, and nearly as astonishing, he surely never expected to hear from the boy's family. Mike told Mark Harris, after hearing the doctor's story, that he was a hero. Mike Miller was a lawyer by training. He knew we lived in a litigious society. He contended that some physicians, for fear of being sued, might have just stayed in their cars, as if Matt were somebody else's problem. Harris told Mike he was no hero, that he was only doing what any doctor would have done, what came naturally to him. He no more could have ignored Matt than an off-duty fireman could have ignored a burning building, or a police officer ignore a crime in progress. Mark Harris said he had done what he was trained to do, the only thing he could do.

"You saved our son's life," Mike Miller said over the phone. "We will always be indebted to you."

"Well, I do have a favor to ask you," Mark Harris said.

"Anything," said Mike.

"I'm going to put my wife on the phone," said Harris, "and can you just tell her everything about Matt that you just told me?"

Mike Miller was an emotional noodle at this point but he talked with Mary Ann Harris for another half hour. There were many more tears of joy.

After the phone call, Mike recounted the conversations to Nancy, Michael and Emily. "That Dr. Harris was in the last car," he told them, "that he was an anesthesiologist, the best person in the world to open an airway, that he was there to save Matt's life – that is plain and simple a miracle."

And speaking of miracles, finally, at 11:56 p.m., at the end of one of the most amazing days of his life, Mike Miller, the greatest thank-you man in mutual fund history, fired off one last note of thanks for the night. To McNabb, Buckley and McIsaac he wrote: "Michael, Nancy and I can't thank you enough for coming down and helping us witness our miracle today... you are wonderful friends and we will never forget your kindness and thought-fulness in coming down today. Keep those prayers coming – we will need them."

CHAPTER FIVE

On Thursday morning, four days after his accident, Matt Miller was awake, more awake than anyone could have expected. If the starting gun of the rest of his life had just gone off, he was out of the blocks in a sprint – a relative sprint. After all, he was still on a mechanical ventilator, which was connected to a tracheotomy tube in his throat that doctors surgically installed Sunday when he arrived. A naso-gastric tube for nutrition was literally pinned to his nose, and ran through his nostril and down his throat into his stomach. His jaw was wired shut. His face was still enormous. He had IVs in both arms, a catheter collecting his urine. His broken right hand had been plated and casted in a surgery the previous afternoon.

Matt was still on heavy, heavy drugs. He indicated to his family and to nurses, somehow, with grunts and gestures, that he wanted to communicate. A therapist brought him an "ICU Talk Device," which looked like a red plastic Etch A Sketch, only it had big square letters like toy typewriter keys. A patient could write words that would appear on the small gray screen. So Matt Miller, on Thursday morning, for the first time since his accident, communicated with the outside world. He typed, ever so slowly, "Can I go to physics lab?"

Was he delusional, or was he serious? The family figured the former, but based on what was to come, perhaps the latter. Matt would have no recollection of writing this. He was probably hallucinating from the combination of his brain injury and his heavy drugs. He also would have no recollection – though Michael always will – of kicking his brother out of the room that afternoon. Michael and Emily were visiting Matt in the ICU together and Matt grunted and gestured with his broken right hand for Michael to get lost, leave. Michael in no way misconstrued Matt's meaning – he wanted to be alone with his girlfriend, to have some privacy, maybe for a quick hug. Michael laughed in wonder and disbelief – the boy was just hours out of a coma – and of course left the room.

In fact, Matt's first memory since high-fiving and eating an energy bar with his fellow riders at Reeds Gap, was that Thursday afternoon, when Michael told his brother he'd see him at Thanksgiving, wherever he happened to be. Michael was in the first semester of his first year in law school and had missed now a week of classes. Hanks had told him that morning it would probably be okay for him to leave and return to his classes. Matt was going to survive, and begin the long, long road of rehabilitation. Dennis Miller, his dad's older brother, was a school teacher in Northern Virginia. He was going to come down, visit Matt in the hospital, and take Michael back to the airport in Washington for an early Friday morning flight. Michael had gone into the room Thursday afternoon to tell Matt goodbye, and that he'd see him at Thanksgiving.

"What are you talking about?" Matt thought to himself. "Of course I'll be home at Thanksgiving." This was the first thing he would remember since the accident, his first memory. He had no idea where he was or what had happened or anything more than thinking everything was normal and of course he'd be home and what was wrong with his brother.

Everything was hardly normal. Matt slept a tremendous amount on Thursday, still under sedation, though out of the coma. The family was still visiting in pairs. After a visit, Emily and Mike were headed back to the waiting room when one of the residents who had been caring for Matt walked by. Emily grabbed him and said, "Matt needs to register for spring classes very soon. Do you think we should go ahead and register for him, just in case?" The resident was taken off guard, and seemed very surprised by her question. He replied, "I am concerned that you may have unreasonable expectations at this point." As soon as the resident walked away, Emily burst into tears and Mike Miller comforted her.

Since the accident, Emily – all of them – had been totally focused on whether Matt would survive. In those first few days, Emily had often asked about worst case scenarios, and in her mind doctors had always been vague, and never given her any. As a result, Emily had just assumed that if Matt were to survive, he'd of course be *Matt*, himself, and their lives would resume like normal. She was clueless and completely naïve, but nobody until that very moment had ever said something so blunt about a possible long-term or permanent brain injury. Now, in a three-second exchange, the veil of ignorance was removed from her eyes. She got her dose of truth from a doctor, and he was just as unprepared to deliver it as she was to receive it. One might think it would be obvious, after such an accident, that life-changing brain injury was a real likelihood. But this came as a complete shock to Emily. Her whole life flashed before her eyes. Would Matt be able to return to college? Would he ever be a doctor? Would he be at home for the rest of his life? She wept in the waiting room and Mike Miller did his best to console her. The Millers had always understood that permanent brain injury was a possibility, even a probability, but truly this wasn't something that they had given much thought to, either. Their entire focus, like Emily's, had been on survival – not on what comes next.

• • •

Ken Gregory lived by himself, and those first few days were difficult. He didn't tell anyone about what happened, not his sister or his mother. He tried to keep busy during the day, to keep his mind off what happened, but those first nights, sleeping was almost impossible. Lying in bed, the images of Matt's cheek hitting his windshield post, or Matt gurgling blood on the road would return full-blown into his mind. Ken took no drugs, saw no doctors. He just sucked it up. He went back to work on Tuesday, and that was rough. Some of the people around the shop had heard about what had happened, and he did answer some of their questions. Mark or Mary Ann called or e-mailed every day at first, to update him about Matt, and to check on him. They called him with the very good news on Thursday, that it appeared Matt was going to make it. But even still, just thinking about what Matt faced, what he'd have to go through if he ever wanted to be himself again, was very hard for Ken. He didn't feel guilty. But he felt responsible. His world had been shaken, much like Matt's brain.

On Friday, Rudy came back to the hospital for a visit, and finally got to see his riding partner. He thought Matt's head was twice the normal size, but he really never expected to see his friend alive again so that didn't really upset him too much. Swollen was much better than dead. Matt had that little typewriter in his lap, and even though he was so clumsy, typing with his broken hand, and kept having to hit backspace, Rudy could finally see the word Matt was trying to type: "What."

"You want to know what happened," Rudy said to Matt. "We'll talk about that some other time."

That Friday, doctors began weaning Matt from the ventilator, and by the weekend he was able to breathe on his own, through his nose and through the open tracheotomy tube in his throat. Because he was off the ventilator, he was able, after seven days, to leave intensive care, and relocate onto Six East, the acute care trauma floor, where patients like Matt typically went after the ICU. A therapist concluded that Matt could safely swallow. So even though his jaw was wired shut, Matt could suck liquid through a straw, and after a week of being entirely fed by a tube through his nose, he sucked down water and juice, and even some clear soup.

Doctors began trying to give the Millers some idea of what lay ahead. He may have permanent brain damage, or perhaps only long-term damage. Matt could be in the hospital for months, depending on his mental and facial recovery, and that would likely be followed by more months in a rehabilitation hospital, to work on memory and speech impairments, personality changes and weaknesses that followed brain injury. The doctors insisted that Mike and Nancy spend time with rehabilitation specialists, who talked to them about Matt having to relearn basic functions, like tying his shoes. There would also inevitably be surprises, complications, possibly some more surgeries. Everyone would have to take it slow, day by day, and see how Matt did. The Millers had notified the Dean of Students about Matt's accident, and everybody pretty much expected that Matt would take incompletes for that fall semester, skip the spring semester altogether as he convalesced, and, God-willing, if possible, he would return to school the following fall.

That was pretty much what everyone thought.

Everyone except Matt.

By Saturday and Sunday, he was literally coming to his senses. On Saturday he was able to get out of bed, and even walk to the bathroom. He learned how to adjust his hospital bed. By Sunday afternoon, after listening to Emily and others, he understood generally what had happened to him, and where he was. He grew impatient with the little ICU talk device, and preferred instead to scribble short, nearly illegible notes with his surgically repaired and casted right hand, in which he was barely able to hold a pen.

Sunday afternoon on a legal pad, fully alert, he scribbled: *"I'm going home for Thanksgiving."*

That would be in 18 days.

His family looked at him with dismay. How could they let him know this was just impossible?

"I'm leaving," he wrote again, *"by Thanksgiving."*

Not one doctor or anyone in his family, or really anybody except Matt himself, believed this to be possible. He kept scribbling notes, "I want out of here," and "home by Thanksgiving."

The doctors explained to the Millers and Emily that Matt just didn't understand what he was facing. Recovery would be six months to a year at least. One of Mike Miller's oldest and best friends, his former law partner from Washington, D.C., Mike Missal, was down visiting on Sunday. He found Matt to be simply unrecognizable and he was thinking to himself this boy would be lucky to go home by Thanksgiving *a year from now.*

Matt began writing more questions:

"How did I get back?"

"Did anyone get my bike?"

To his mother: "Can you look for chicken broth with lower sodium?"

Nobody understood. They all had just been through the worst week of their lives. Matt might die. Matt might live, but would he ever be himself?

But Matt had not experienced any of that. The past week, in some ways, was literally not in his head. In fact, he was still feeling pretty high, relatively speaking. His last conscious memories were good ones – the wonderful week at school, cycling up the mountain. And when he woke up in the hospital, he ran through a checklist in his mind, and felt good. His mind was working. His legs were working. He just looked at this accident as a minor interruption in his life. He couldn't do triathlons for another month. Big deal. He didn't think he was doing so bad, and so it didn't seem unusual or crazy to him to think he could go to the Corner, the college strip just across from the hospital, and get a milkshake, or go home. He had no real awareness of how close he'd come to death, or how grave his injuries were.

Mike Miller pointed out to one doctor all the things that Matt was doing – writing notes with perfect spelling, monitoring what he was eating. Didn't that suggest his brain was fine? The doctor was somewhat dismissive, replying, "We'll know when he does something really challenging, like take a physics exam."

On Tuesday, November 11, nine days after the accident, Emily brought her laptop computer with her to the hospital, which had wireless internet. That evening, Matt, using Emily's computer, tried to log into the UVA computer system. Emily was fully aware of what Matt was attempting to do, but Mike and Nancy were not. They were sitting in the room with him but didn't realize what was happening. Matt was attempting to register for spring classes. Emily may not have been so crazy four days earlier to have suggested it. Insane as it might have seemed at that moment to his parents and his doctors, Matt was thinking that of course he'd be taking classes that spring, that his life was going to return to normal, and Emily was just following Matt's lead in terms of outlook and expectations. Matt's parents didn't want to upset him, or discourage him, so they didn't make a big deal of it at that moment. But they were clearly troubled. Therapists had told them their son might need to learn how to tie his shoes again, so how could Matt think about taking classes, much less pre-med physics? Matt couldn't log on that night, the system was down, but he was undeterred by that inconvenience or by his parents' concerns. After he closed Emily's laptop, Matt wrote a note to his father, asking him to swing by Montebello Circle and pick up his books for school. He wanted to begin catching up on his work.

• • •

Matt's dad had returned to Vanguard for a couple days, the previous Sunday and Monday, and would toggle back and forth over the next few weeks between Vanguard and the hospital. His focus was always Matt. In fact, on that Sunday, the 9th, a week after the accident, he e-mailed Matt: *"I flew home today but will be back with you soon. Mom and Emily told me you walked out to the terrace. You continue to amaze everyone! I love you very, very much. I told you this last night and I'm going to tell you again – you are the toughest, bravest person I have ever known...."*

Mike Miller had enormous responsibilities back at work. Matt's accident happened during the heart of the financial crisis. The markets were in free fall, and the government was in free fall around it. The world was on the brink of financial meltdown. On top of that, Mike had a new boss – McNabb, who had just replaced Brennan as CEO. Mike's role at Vanguard had really been custom designed – anything that didn't quite fit somewhere else Jack Brennan had assigned to him as the company grew because Mike had the breadth and range to manage it: security, portfolio review, government relations, new fund launches, compliance, information security, communications and marketing. And when big decisions were made, Mike was the one who always worried most about the Vanguard brand and integrity associated with the name. Mike's team certainly stepped up in his absence, but Mike Miller stayed connected and the work got done. "He stayed involved in big decisions and I tell you it was amazing how he balanced everything," said McNabb. "I give him a ton of credit. I don't really know how he did it. We had a lot of tough stuff going on, and Mike's voice was important and it always seemed to be there when we needed it."

Mike was back at his office for a day or two at a time, and often had to send his administrative assistant, Nancy Ruffini, to get him something to eat from the cafeteria. If he would go himself, he would continually get stopped by friends and coworkers expressing condolences or making inquiries about Matt – the whole company, it seemed, was getting Nancy Ruffini's daily updates – and Mike realized quickly he couldn't get his work done if he stopped to talk to them all. This was very hard for Mike because he was naturally gregarious and so grateful for the well-wishes of his colleagues, but he needed to do his work quickly and get back to Charlottesville, where he really wanted to be.

Nancy took a leave from her job as an archivist at the University of Pennsylvania, and settled in at the Marriott Courtyard, across from the hospital, for the long haul. This was why she had wisely conserved her energy, contained her emotions, as if she had known from the very beginning that she was at the start of a very long journey. Beginning Saturday, November 8, she kept a notebook of everything going on involved in Matt's recovery – which doctors came by, what they said, which tests he had, who visited him. She tried to be at the hospital by 6:00 a.m., so she could talk with the doctors stopping by Matt's room on their morning rounds. Nancy had come to Charlottesville for a weekend. She had packed only two skirts, a vest, two blouses, and of course her swim suit and goggles that she took with her anytime she ever traveled. The first week and a half, until Mike was able to bring her back a few more things, she just wore the same two blouses and skirts over and over, washing them at the hotel and wearing them again. Nobody was looking at her, and it didn't matter if they were. Who really cared what you looked like when your son was fighting for his life? Now that Matt was out of the ICU, and beginning what felt like a new phase – the long and winding road to recovery – Nancy made it a point to swim every day. That she would do for herself. She didn't know it but the first rule in caregiving is care for the caregiver. She would be of little use to Matt unless she kept herself sharp and managed the stress, and for her a daily swim was the way to do it. The Marriott had an indoor pool. Nothing fancy but good enough for her. She swam half a mile every day, freestyle, open turns. At age 55, her days of doing flip turns were far behind her.

She and Mike pretty much insisted that Emily go back to classes, which she did, but Emily usually brought her books to Matt's room and spent the day there studying and just being with Matt when she wasn't in class. When Emily arrived, Nancy often used that as an opportunity to take a walk, or do some shopping for Matt, picking up a peanut butter milkshake for him to suck down from Ben & Jerry's or some other high-calorie drinks. The hospital room was freezing and so one afternoon early in that second week she ran over to the Harris Teeter grocery store and bought a blanket. The cashier asked her in a pleasant, Southern, making-conversation kind-of-way, what the blanket was for, and Nancy, answered honestly: her son had nearly died in a bicycle accident and it was freezing in his hospital room. The cashier opened her pocket book, pulled out her prayer book, and asked Nancy for her son's name, so she could write it down and pray for him. Nancy thanked her and obliged.

Matt was simply astonishing. A week after emerging from a pharmacologically-induced coma, ten days after sustaining what the medical record officially called parenchymal shear injury, contusions, intraventricular hemorrhage, and subdural hematoma, doctors came in to Matt's room that Wednesday morning to find him reading his physics textbook.

This was truly just mind-blowing to these doctors, who of course thought they had seen it all. In fact, in all honesty, his behavior alarmed them. Sheehan, the neurosurgeon, was concerned that all this reading and studying was going to tax him, exhaust him, and be too much of a strain on his recovering brain. Sheehan would have been immensely pleased just to see somebody who had been through what Matt had to be sitting up in bed. That would be a triumph. But studying physics? *Using a highlighter?*

"You could see it in their faces," Mike Miller said. "Doctors would be blown away by that." Sheehan just literally scratched his head the first few times he saw it, tried to suggest to Matt that maybe he wanted to slow down, take it easy. But Sheehan began to see this was therapeutic for Matt, and became more supportive.

And then there was the issue, frankly, of Matt's face. He looked like a stroke victim. Not only was he still prodigiously swollen, but it was clear now that he had suffered extensive nerve damage in the accident. Nerves controlling the left side of his face simply didn't work. He couldn't close his left eye, and doctors had inserted a gold weight into his left eyelid, to enlist the aid of gravity. This was another surgery. His mouth zigzagged like a plunging stock-market table. He was drooling. He couldn't smile. There was no way of knowing at this point if his nerves would ever work again, or if so, to what degree. Matthew Miller had been a healthy, handsome college student and now he looked visibly deformed. There was no way to sugarcoat it. Yet this fact didn't appear to bother Matt in the slightest.

Dr. Jared Christophel, the chief resident working with Dr. Park, would come into Matt's room every morning, sometimes even before 6:00 a.m., to check on his patient. Matt, assorted tubes in tow, would get out of bed, walk toward the door, and, with his casted paw, shake Dr. Christophel's hand. "Get back in bed!" the doctor would order. Christophel was still a relatively young doctor, a fifth-year resident, but he had never seen such a thing before. A patient, one as injured as Matt, had every right to be so thoroughly depressed and withdrawn, to lament what he had just lost, to be devastated by the enormity of what had happened to him, to rage at the world, or at least want to withdraw from it. But to get out of bed to shake the doctor's hand? Christophel was blown away. And Matt was always cheerful and pleasant and so positive. Matt was in fact so positive that Park and Christophel worried about him. He had such obvious physical and facial defects, and such uncertainties about his future, that it was normal and expected for him to go through a grieving period of his own, to experience anger and sadness. Dr. Park at first honestly thought that Matt's positive behavior and attitude was an obvious consequence of his brain injury, a personality disorder, a sure sign that his brain wiring had been damaged and his emotional responses were irrational. A brain injury was the likeliest explanation for his behavior. But after a few days, and more interaction with Matt, and more observation, Park decided that this wasn't the case. But Christophel was still so concerned about Matt's behavior – believing Matt was bottling up his true feelings inside and this could ultimately be very harmful – that he twice spoke privately to Nancy in the hallway, expressing his concern. Nancy wasn't worried about this. She was beginning to understand her son's mettle. This was just who he was.

Even Matt's friends who knew him as a positive person were stunned. Chris Morrow went in to see him for the first time a week after the accident, and he walked into the room to find Matt reading a *triathlon magazine*. Matt, granted, had no recollection of the actual accident. This was common with trauma patients, and in particular head injury patients. Matt's inability to remember the actual accident, Dr. Sheehan explained, was caused by a combination of the injury to his brain and also by the drugs used to induce the coma, which had an "amnestic effect." Sheehan thought the emotional horror of being in the accident – and the brain trying to block it out – probably had little or no influence on the amnesia. Chris Morrow, however, had all too vivid a memory. And he could also see clearly the pain on the faces of Matt's parents, a pain he never wanted to cause his own family, which is why he had decided to sell his bike, give up triathlons and stick to running and swimming.

Matt, also, was all too well aware of the pain he'd caused his family and Emily. And that's part of the reason he wasn't even thinking about his face, and didn't seem concerned about it. It was the strangest thing – a disconnect – to have no memory, no emotional connection to an event that caused everyone you love immense pain. But Matt wanted more than anything else in life to somehow remedy and atone for this great hurt he'd cause them. And he could see that what healed them the most, and helped them the most, was to see him thrive. And he wasn't going to let anything get in the way of that. In all honesty, had his family not been there for him, had Emily not been there for him, Matt probably wouldn't have been nearly as motivated, nearly as determined. But they were there for him. And their greatest tonic was seeing Matt thrive. And the best way he could repay them was to be positive, and to get out of the hospital as fast as possible. He was being selfless and selfish at the same time. What was best for him was best for them – get well and get out. He couldn't allow himself to go negative, because that would have been another crushing blow to those who loved him. And he just couldn't allow that.

But if Matt seemed so positive and confident by day, night was another story.

During the day, Matt was busy. Friends came constantly. He became unbeatable at the card game, rummy. He had doctors coming in constantly for one thing or another. He was reading. Everyone around him was positive, and he was feeding off that. The feeding tube down his throat didn't bother him that much during the day because he had so many other things to occupy his thoughts. Some days, honestly, maybe even for a few hours, he'd forget that he was even in the hospital because he was having such a good time visiting with friends.

But nights were different. Nights were long, and lonely. He couldn't sleep well. His face was so swollen he had to elevate his bed to 45 degrees, which made sleeping even harder. The feeding tube was a constant irritation, literally. The beeps and noises were incessant and so unnerving at night. He would press the call button every hour, at least, and ask the nurse for a drink of water, just for some company. He had no way to occupy himself. He'd literally count the hours until morning, and one of the reasons he was so pleased to see Dr. Christophel so early each day was that his arrival signaled relief from these lonely, horrible nights. Most of the notes Matt wrote declaring he was going home, or wanted out of the hospital, were all written in the morning, early, soon after his mother arrived, when he still felt this desperation most strongly.

Even in these lowest moments, in the darkest, loneliest of nights, Matt never once cursed his fate, or rued what had happened to him. He was angry, sure, furious that he was still in the hospital. He thought he was well enough to leave, and didn't need to be there, and was livid that everyone else simply didn't understand this. He was furious they made him stay. But even in his lowest moments, in those loneliest of nights, he didn't stew or brood over what had put him in this spot. He didn't mourn over what he'd lost. He didn't curse his fate. And this was simply because of the most practical and pragmatic of reasons, because of who Matt was and how he viewed the world: What good would it do? Dwelling on his misfortune wouldn't change anything. Wallowing would only make things worse – and that was in direct conflict with his prime directive: to get better and go home. Matt had nothing against deep thinking, or ruminating in general, but only when productive.

His take from the hospital bed, and about life in general, was simple, really: When thinking helps you, think all you want. But when thinking doesn't help you, what's the use of thinking?

Still, nights in the hospital were horrible for him. And he kept that misery to himself for a while. But it revealed itself in two stages – first through temporary insanity, and then through a very conscious plea for help.

At 2:00 a.m. on Wednesday, November 12, Matt texted Emily to "turn off the stove and put away the groceries." That morning, nurses told Emily that Matt was often confused in the night, perhaps from the brain injury or from the narcotics he was taking for pain. This was eye-opening to Emily. She had naively assumed that he was just sleeping peacefully through the night. The next night at 1:00 a.m., Matt texted, "I miss you." Emily knew her boyfriend well enough to know that he hated imposing on anyone, even her, and this message really meant that he was very lonely, maybe even scared, and he needed her. She knew now that Matt was suffering in the evenings and didn't want him to go through that alone. So she ran from her dorm to the hospital, close to a mile, in the middle of the night. When she got there, his eyes were moist. She spent the night in a chair, moving it as close to his bed as she could. They just held hands as he lay there. He wouldn't let go, and Emily knew he just wanted to be sure that she was still there. She came back night after night, but always tried to leave before 6:00, returning the chair to its normal position, so Matt's mother never found out.

• • •

When Matt was still in the ICU, Kelly O'Donnell, the nutritionist attached to the trauma unit, went into his room to do an assessment. Emily greeted her that first time and they were chatting and Emily told her, "You know, Matt's an athlete and has less than five percent body fat." And O'Donnell, with 19 years of experience, was thinking to herself, "Yeah, right. We don't have *any* patient with less than five percent body fat." O'Donnell was sure this silly undergraduate had no idea what she was talking about. Nutritionists at the University of Virginia hospital and in hospitals all over America were confronted constantly by the opposite problem – a sea of obesity. But when O'Donnell took a look at Matt in bed, and saw the six-pack of muscles on his abdomen, and examined his medical records, she could see without actually measuring his body fat index that Emily had been right or very close to it. This young man was *fit*.

And that created a different problem. Matt would need an extraordinary amount of calories to recover. The body's physiological response to such extreme trauma is to produce many extra hormones needed for healing. That, in turn, causes the body's energy expenditure rate to soar. To create these additional hormones used in healing increased the body's need for calories – fuel – by at least 50 percent. The need for calories is even greater for athletes. In Matt's case, he had no body fat stored, no source of extra calories. The danger was that if he didn't get the calories he needed, his body would begin consuming its own muscle. Rather than heal, he would deteriorate.

As soon as Matt had left the ICU, and moved to the trauma floor, O'Donnell went to see Nancy about his nutritional needs. She explained the situation and said Matt needed 4,000 calories a day, an extraordinary amount. The nutritionist said Matt was going to need a feeding tube surgically implanted through his abdomen right into his stomach. This was known as a PEG tube. High calorie liquids – like Ensure – could be pumped directly into his stomach. The feeding tube through Matt's nose and down his throat was a very short-term measure, the nutritionist said. Matt couldn't leave the hospital with it. The stomach tube would be more long term, and could be used in a rehabilitation hospital or even at home. And in O'Donnell's mind – as surely as the sun rises in the east – Matt was going to need a PEG tube for months, certainly until he could get some temporary teeth and chew actual food. "He cannot eat 4,000 calories through a straw," O'Donnell told Nancy. "I think he needs a tube in his stomach."

Nancy Miller was quite adamant. No. She discussed the subject with her son, and felt this would devastate him, and she wasn't about to let that happen. He'd been through enough. Matt told his mother he believed he could suck down enough calories, increasing the volume gradually, so that he could reach 4,000 calories a day by Thanksgiving. In Matt's mind, if in nobody else's, this was an achievable goal.

O'Donnell reacted to Nancy Miller in much the same way as she had reacted to Emily – this woman has *no idea*. But O'Donnell recognized an immoveable force when she ran into one, and agreed to let Matt give it a try – one week. See if he could get his calories up. Nancy, or Mark Bernardino, every day brought Matt the Ben & Jerry's peanut-butter milkshake. Matt also began sipping two 440-calorie protein shakes the hospital provided him. But in bed one morning, he read the ingredients: "trans fat 3g." "That's it," Matt wrote. "No more of these shakes for me." He replaced them with orange-flavored Breeze, a juice box with 250 calories and 9 grams of protein. He started out with two a day and steadily increased. Friends on the swim team hunted through their locker room for high protein drinks, also rich in calories, and brought them over. Matt McLean and another swimmer went over to the Harris Teeter to buy cases of the highest calorie drink they could find. When they were in line to pay, the cashier, just being conversational, asked them what they were going to do with all these drinks. They told her their classmate, in the hospital after a horrible bike accident, had his jaw wired shut and could only suck down liquids through a straw. The cashier asked them if their friend's name was Matt Miller. They were stunned by this. "He's already in my prayer book," she told them, "and I'm praying for him every day."

Nancy Miller kept a log of everything Matt drank, her own personal medical record, and O'Donnell came by daily to check it. And every day the calorie count was rising.

• • •

Matt was fortunate in so many ways – not only had he survived the accident, and appeared to have avoided permanent brain injury, but he was nourished by a loving family and a daily regimen of visitors. Dr. Hanks, who dropped by almost daily, noted that "you needed a ticket to get in." Jena Brenton, one of the nurses on the acute care trauma wing taking care of Matt, felt every time she went into his room there was a friend or family member at his side. Michael, back in California, video-chatted with Matt pretty much every evening. This was the idea of Michael's girlfriend, Linda Liu. Linda would use her Mac laptop, which had a camera, and Matt would use Emily's Mac, with its camera. The brothers could see one another and chat. Chat was a relative term. Michael would talk and Matt would grunt, or give his brother a thumbs-up or thumbs-down.

Mark Bernardino, the Virginia swim coach, had been coming by to see Matt every day, sometimes twice a day. On Wednesday, November 12, he brought Matt a present, a T-shirt.

"I'm tired of seeing you in a hospital gown," Bernardino said.

On the shirt was a quote from North Carolina State basketball coach Jimmy Valvano, shortly before he died of cancer:

Don't give up, don't ever give up. How do you go from where you are to where you want to be? I think you have to have an enthusiasm for life. You have to have a dream, a goal, and you have to be willing to work for it."

Bernardino did something else that day. He got Matt out of bed and walked with him down the hall. The next day he was back and they walked down two hallways and back. The next day they headed into the stairwell. On November 15, Bernardino walked down and then back up two flights of stairs with Matt. On Sunday, November 16, two weeks after the accident, Bernardino walked Matt from his sixth floor hospital room, up two flights to the eighth floor, down to the first floor, and six flights back up to Matt's room. The day after that, Bernardino's calves were "on fire." Matt was fine. Bernardino could see how much Matt was loving this, how he relished the challenge each day, finding a way to be competitive, to test the limits of his own endurance and then expand them.

In a very real sense, Bernardino had become Matt's coach again.

Bernardino happened to have at that moment about 60 other students to coach – the men's and women's swim teams were entering the heart of their season. Virginia was a regional and national swimming power, with several swimmers on both squads with Olympic potential. Matt Miller had swum for Bernardino for only one year, and walked away. And that was nearly two years ago. Yet Bernardino was in that hospital every day. He broke into tears one afternoon when Matt scribbled him a note, "I love you Dino. Thanks for being here." Bernardino hung it on his office wall.

Bernardino had swum for UVA himself, back in the early 1970s. He was also from the Philadelphia area, Upper Darby, a blue-collar town right outside the city. He loved competing and swimming, and he found after he graduated from UVA, and was two years into the business world, he missed swimming and competing terribly. He came back to UVA in graduate school, and was working as an assistant coach on the side, for $1,000 a year. When the head coaching job opened up suddenly, he took it at the age of 26. Now 56 and vastly wiser, he could say with honesty that he wasn't ready back then, wasn't prepared. He felt badly that his swimmers and divers those first few years didn't get the quality coaching they deserved. They helped him learn how to be a head coach. He was a hard ass, and in particular back then because the age difference was so slight, he had to make it his way or the highway. He had to be ironhanded. In time as he grew, he learned, and his coaching philosophy boiled down to two fundamental tenets. The first, find out what motivates each kid and push him as much as he can be pushed. Bernardino believed in hard work, and the benefits of hard work. Whether in the pool or in the board room or in a marriage or raising kids or whatever challenges would lay ahead, if these swimmers could tough it out at his practices, do what he demanded, then he believed they would be prepared for the challenges that lay ahead, far beyond swimming, and that's what he told them. They would have discipline and confidence and staying power. His second tenet was simply to love the kids, to care about them deeply, to let them know he cared about them far beyond the edge of the pool, and that he would be there for them in time of need. That's what he tried to show them.

By the time Michael Miller arrived as a first year student, Bernardino had built UVA swimming into a conference and national power, and the average member of the team was a much better swimmer than Michael. Yet Michael went to Bernardino's office a few weeks after school started his first-year and asked the coach if he could be a walk-on. Michael Miller believed there wasn't another Division I swimming program in America where he could have walked into the coach's office, told him his times, and "not be laughed right out of the office." But Michael believes that Bernardino "has this old school Horatio Alger view that people can pull themselves up, and a walk-on represents that, and he embraces it."

Bernardino told Michael at that first meeting that he'd give him a chance, but that Michael needed to find a niche, a way to help the team. Bernardino knew by Michael's times and Michael knew by his times that he would never be able to help the team by winning races and scoring points. He'd have to find some other way, or he wouldn't be able to stay.

Michael Miller gave that team all he had. Though others were more talented, nobody worked harder in practices. Nobody had a more positive attitude. Michael, scrawny as they come, immediately received the nickname *Sticks* from his much more herculean teammates, and Bernardino loved throwing all he could at this 140-pound weakling in workouts and seeing him thrive. It showed the superstars that if this kid could get through these practices without whining, without quitting, they could, too. Michael loved that Bernardino treated him just like everyone else, yelled at him just like everyone else, and this in fact made him just like everyone else on the team. The other swimmers followed Bernardino's example. Michael was expected to improve and reach the times that Bernardino set for him, just like anyone else. "It helped me swim better but it also gave me an incredible amount of self belief," Michael said of his experience with Bernardino. "If you have somebody that believes in you and sets high expectations and holds you accountable, that gives you an enormous amount of confidence. In high school I was quiet and studied a lot, definitely wasn't nearly as outgoing or taking on a leadership role like I do now, and that change had everything to do with Mark. He encouraged me to be more vocal on the pool deck. He developed my character traits as much as he developed my swimming potential."

While teammates called him Sticks, Bernardino called Michael Miller "Mr. President." Michael was smart, 4.0-gpa, and he fulfilled his niche to the team first by becoming a hard worker, and then a leader. He was a great listener, and he knew quickly and easily how to find out who was having a bad time with school, or with a girl, or who was down on his own performances, and he knew how to lift kids up. He was great in the locker room, helping to resolve the friction that inevitably developed among strong personalities under the stress of a competitive college sport. Michael was a walk-on who was elected team captain his fourth year by his teammates.

When Matt showed up on team, also as a walk-on, Bernardino saw these exact same qualities. Matt had such spirit, was so positive, and such a hard worker. He was dedicated to his teammates, and such a nice kid. Bernardino, in fact, saw more potential as a swimmer in Matt than he did in Michael, which made Bernardino even more excited to have Matt on the team. Matt Miller met all of Bernardino's expectations that first year. But unlike his brother, Matt didn't love swimming. Frankly, he was bored. He just didn't have the same passion for the sport that his brother did. And he wanted to be really great at a sport and he knew swimming was never going to be it. Matt gave the team 100 percent, but when his first season ended, he told his parents and his coach he was quitting.

Bernardino was upset, and told Matt he was making a big mistake. He tried in his most intimidating way – using his hot Italian temper, his Philly streetwise toughness and the intimidation of his coaching position all to persuade Matt to stay on the team. He even sought advice from Michael, who wisely and honestly told Bernardino that if someone doesn't really love swimming, putting in all those miles and making such a huge sacrifice is really a very hard thing to ask of them. So Matt walked away. But Bernardino never got angry, or wrote off Matt, or closed the book on him. Many coaches might have. But Bernardino told Matt the door was always open. He would always be welcomed back on the team. And Bernardino held no grudge. He told Matt to stay in touch, feel free to come by anytime, and contact him should he ever need anything. And by the fall of Matt's third year, after Matt had discovered triathlons, he was back in the pool two, three or four mornings a week, training on his own during open swims, when any student could use the pool. And Matt would always stop by Bernardino's office, talking about his times, his workouts. Bernardino was impressed by his enthusiasm. Bernardino could see a spark in Matt he didn't see that first year on the swim team. He could see Matt had found what he was searching for. Bernardino also came to one other conclusion. He had Matt figured all wrong. He had thought Matt was a sprinter, and seeing him in the water that fall, hearing about his workouts on the bike and on the track, seeing how quickly he recovered from one day to the next, Bernardino realized he had blown it. This was not the easiest thing for him to admit. Matt was no sprinter. He was a natural endurance athlete, and Bernardino felt he should have seen it.

So when Bernardino heard, coming home from his son's soccer game, that Matt was in the hospital, he had to be there. He'd like to think he would have been there for any swimmer or former swimmer who needed the same support. And now that, in the hospital, he had become Matt's coach again, he was as amazed as anyone, day after day, how Matt was able to respond, and recover, and drive himself.

"I honestly don't think very many people could have lived through his trauma," said Bernardino. "His engine was so powerful, his lungs, his heart, his mind. I call that the engine of an athlete. They were so tuned, so fit, so ready for battle. He thought his battle would be a triathlon. And he found himself unexpectedly in the battle for his life."

Bernardino could also see the doctors and nurses watching Matt with disbelief and how that was having such an enormously positive effect on Matt. "Matt could feel their joy and excitement at what he was doing medically," Bernardino said. "He was making them shake their heads, and he was loving it."

• • •

At the time Matt wasn't thinking lofty thoughts, about determination or drive or honor or motivation. He was thinking one raw, simple, primal thought. He wanted out. He hated the bed pan and being helped to the bathroom. He hated sponge baths by strangers. He hated the medications that made him loopy. He hated the noises and interruptions. He hated a feeding tube clipped to his nose and running down his throat. He hated the loss of control. He hated the roommate who blasted the TV. He hated the nights. He was eternally and profoundly grateful for the medical care that had saved his life, and that was helping him to recover now. But he hated, *hated* being in the hospital and being a patient. He was a fabulous patient, a doctor's dream – so willing and compliant and responsible, so devoted to his recovery. Matt's positive attitude and outlook wasn't an act, and it wasn't a decision. It was more a God-given tool, like the tail fin on a tuna, which he was going to use to get where he had to go – and that was out of the hospital. That was his entire focus. Out by Thanksgiving. He wrote it in notes to his family so many times he might have considered getting a tattoo, were he the tattooing kind, and were it possible in the hospital. Whatever it took, sucking down a million calories, he was leaving. And not going to any nursing home or rehabilitation hospital. He was going *home. By Thanksgiving.*

At least that's what he thought.

———

CHAPTER SIX

After that first week, when it became clearer that Matt would not only live but at least in some ways be himself, it also became clear that he had suffered extensive nerve damage to his face. This was becoming a grave concern. The facial nerve that controls the left side of the face comes from the brain, passing the left temple area, and then splits into five branches, controlling everything from the forehead to the chin. Matt would need this facial nerve to furrow his brow, close his eye, to smile – essentially to make all his facial expressions on the left half of his face. Matt's facial nerve wasn't working anywhere – all five branches were down. Was the main trunk, feeding all five branches, severed – perhaps cut by the jagged broken jaw bone? Was it pulverized by the blunt force – literally just disintegrating on impact? Or was that main trunk just stretched to the point of extreme injury, and temporarily out of order, but would in time heal itself? The same questions could be asked of each individual branch – disconnected and never coming back or just temporarily out of service? Facial nerves can regenerate. But if severed, disconnected, they can't reattach on their own. That would require surgery.

Doctors Park and Christophel also knew that if the nerves were severed or crushed to the point of breaking, the window to find these disconnected nerves, and try to restore them, to reconnect them, was three weeks. If they didn't rewire them within three weeks, give or take a few days, Matt's nerve function, were it indeed severed, would be lost and gone forever. He would never be able to go into a Starbucks again without people staring.

Had Park and Christophel known that Matt had no facial nerve function when they did their original reconstruction, on the evening of the accident, they likely would have conducted an exploration, searching for severed facial nerves to reconnect. But they didn't expect Matt to experience "facial nerve paralysis" – the medical term for what he now had – because he didn't seem like a candidate for it. He didn't have any lacerations of the flesh from the injury, which was simply extraordinary in its own right. But without obvious rips or cuts to the flesh, there was nothing to suggest the nerves would have been severed. And trying to find and restore severed facial nerves was generally a very risky enterprise, often causing more harm than benefit. Park said these facial nerves were not only incredibly small and hard to see, but had the texture of "wet toilet paper," and were easily ripped. It would be possible that in their effort to find broken nerves and repair them, surgeons could unknowingly damage healthy ones, and make a face that might recover on its own permanently disfigured.

In any case, that initial surgery had come and gone. But as they considered the question of whether to explore his facial nerves at this point, almost two weeks after the accident, it also became clear that doctors would need to do a second major facial surgery on Matt, anyway. This was not unusual. In the days since Matt's original surgery, his face had fallen slightly out of alignment. This was to be expected as still vibrant muscles pushed and pulled and adjusted to the new titanium frame. If Matt ever wanted to have a chance to have dentures or dental implants that would line up, a jaw that would function properly, and a face that would look natural in shape, he would need surgical modification of his alignment by Park. So there was a consideration that perhaps when they did this realignment surgery, Park and Christophel could also explore the nerve damage. This was a decision Matt and his family faced.

And then there was a third and perhaps the most dangerous complication of all. On the original CT scans, doctors noticed that the carotid artery on Matt's left side, a primary vessel that provides blood to the brain, had been damaged in the crash. Again, the jaw bone, or some bone in Matt's face, had slammed into the artery with incredible force. Dr. Calland, the trauma surgeon, compared this to smashing a garden hose with a sledge hammer. What resulted was a bubble, a weakness, known as an aneurysm. In the very first scans, doctors noted it but it seemed minor, something to watch. But alarmingly, in subsequent scans, the bubble was growing and getting worse. If the bubble burst, or even leaked, Matt would suffer certain stroke and likely death. This was not a risk anyone was willing to take. The neurosurgeons wanted to put a stent inside this damaged artery, a wire mesh fortification, which would act like a brace, and would remain permanently.

Now if doctors did the stent procedure first – Matt would need to remain for several months on heavy blood thinners to prevent any clotting and to make sure the stent incorporated itself smoothly into the artery. But doing the stent procedure first, and following with the required blood thinners, would force the delay for months of the second facial surgery. A facial surgery to the degree they were planning would cause immense bleeding. And if Matt were on a heavy dose of blood thinners, that would be just too dangerous. But if they postponed the facial surgery for months, until Matt was off the thinners, all the bones in his face would have set, and this option would require breaking and resetting several bones in his face. This would be not only painful but raise another set of risks.

With all these issues emerging, to Matt's family and physicians, getting discharged by Thanksgiving not only seemed even more unrealistic and impossible, but much less important.

• • •

This was a harrowing and nerve-wracking time for the Millers, akin to those first few days when Matt faced life or death. Things had been going along so well. Matt was shocking everyone with his progress and positive attitude. In fact, Mike Miller e-mailed his friends at Vanguard that staffers around the hospital were referring to his son as "Miracle Matt," because he was walking and writing and reading and recovering so quickly after brain injury. Doctors who weren't even involved in his care would come by to meet him, just to see for themselves. Matt now faced more surgeries – each of them major, with the most serious implications. Each by itself would be a matter for worry. But being in conflict with one another – having to decide which one to do first, weighing the risks – only ramped up the stress and tension. Do the stent first and let the facial bones harden out of alignment? Or realign the face, but risk a stroke? What about exploration of the facial nerves? The clock was ticking on that.

Matt, alert, was now an active participant in discussions about his medical care. He seemed to be the least stressed among his family and Emily. He had complete faith in his doctors. They saved his life, helped him get this far. He trusted them to do the right thing, whatever it was.

Nancy knew what she wanted. "I'm willing to take the risk," she told the doctors. This was the first time she really felt exhausted, completely drained. "I know you may think I'm terrible," she told one resident. "I fully understand what could happen if he were to have a stroke. I understand. But it's been like two weeks. I really don't think it's any worse today than yesterday. I'm going to take the risk of 24 hours and see if they can align that jaw first."

Frankly, this was not a decision the family was going to make unilaterally. If the doctors felt it would be unsafe, that the risk of stroke were too high, they would never allow the facial surgery to come first. This was a situation where Calland, Sheehan, Park and Christophel and others conferred, examined the patient, the scans, the tests, weighed their options using their soundest professional judgment, and made the call. They told the Millers they would meet with them to make a final decision on Thursday morning, November 18.

Mike Miller summarized the family's agony in an e-mail at 6:32 a.m. to Jack Brennan: "We're praying the facial surgery can go ahead as planned.... This is the toughest decision we've faced. It was a tough night..."

The doctors were unanimous: the stent could wait a few days. Park was given the go ahead to do the facial realignment. Park then decided against searching for a severed facial nerve at the same time. He wanted to err on the side of caution.

Park had been surprised from the start that all five nerves were out of order. He knew it was extremely rare that blunt force trauma – even the full-on facial smash that Matt endured – would crush the nerves so much they would just disintegrate and fail to heal on their own. He knew these nerves were amazingly resilient, despite being so whispery thin. He wanted to go ahead with the second facial surgery, restore the alignment, and continue in the days that followed with more testing of the facial nerves. There were tests doctors could perform that would determine conductivity. If doctors could find some indication of life, of conductivity, that would rule out exploratory surgery for severed nerves. And if they could not find any life, if it seemed surgery was the only hope for repair, Park believed they still had time. He felt that even after the stent procedure, he could explore the facial nerve, blood thinners notwithstanding.

Back into the operating room Matt went on Wednesday, November 19, five more hours of surgery on his face. Mike e-mailed Jack Brennan at 9:59 p.m.: "Seeing Matt lying there afterward, with the swelling and trauma from yet another round of having his face reworked, really brought home the severity of his injuries and what he's been through…"

Two days after that, on Friday, November 21, surgeons put the stent in Matt's carotid artery. Using a stent to fix an aneurysm in the carotid artery was a relatively new procedure, less than ten years old. It carried its own measure of danger, but was deemed safer than surgical repair or bypass. The actual aneurysm was located high on his carotid artery, near the brain stem, a very hard place to reach surgically and no place to fool around. The bubble was within the walls of the artery, and technically called a pseudo aneurysm, but if it burst or leaked, the consequences would be just as lethal. The amount of blood flowing through the carotid artery is astronomically high compared with other vessels in the body, Sheehan said. The brain gets more blood than any other organ, and even a slight reduction in blood flow leads to a stroke. The stent entered Matt's body through his groin, and was guided by doctors through his arteries until it reached the damaged location. Then the little wire mesh stent was released, almost like the opening of a parachute. It formed a brace, shoring up the weakened artery, removing stress on it and giving the aneurysm time to heal. The mesh would become interwoven with the artery in time, and was intended to be permanent. But the technology was relatively new, and no one could be sure just how long it would last should Matt live into old age. Sheehan said Matt would need regular scans of that carotid artery all his life and he would also need to take medicine to make sure his platelets didn't get too sticky, which was different from clotting. Taking such medicine was routine procedure after a stent and shouldn't affect his daily living.

The procedure seemed to go well, without any surprises or complications. Matt went back into intensive care for at least a night, maybe more, as a precaution.

"We're no longer optimistic about getting out of here by Thanksgiving," Mike Miller e-mailed Brennan that Friday night, November 21. "But that's okay. We're incredibly grateful to be where we are. And to have made the progress that we've made. So makes no difference where we are – we'll have much to celebrate."

• • •

By the next afternoon, that Saturday, Matt was back to Six East, the acute care trauma wing, "his home away from home," as the family called it.

The conversation turned to his facial nerves, the next issue to address. For the very first time since the accident, Matt Miller looked at himself in the mirror. This was truly the first time he took a good long look.

"I look fine Mom," he wrote.

"Well, your smile's a bit off," she replied with loving understatement.

"Isn't my smile fine?" he asked Emily.

"Well, not really," she said. "It's okay, though."

Nancy Miller was certain at that moment she saw a trace of fear in her son's eyes. She might even have seen tears beginning to well, though she wasn't sure, and no tear ever rolled down his cheek at that moment, or any moment as far as she knew. And the fear she saw was only a flicker. Matt may never have wanted to admit it, and may not even have realized he felt it, but it was there. Nancy was sure of it. A nurse came into the room, and told Matt she'd seen patients like him before and their nerves had come back, and his should come back, too. The nurse told him to just wait and see. If Matt were momentarily sinking in spirit and outlook, this nurse and her optimism had snapped him right back into a positive frame of mind.

Matt had a very different take on that moment than his mother. He wasn't upset by what he saw in the mirror. It wasn't that he didn't care how he looked – he did. This was a young man who earned the nickname Sleeves because he loved showing off his biceps. And in fact, before the accident he'd get upset about a pimple on his face. But his world was different now. He was so rooted in the present, in the moment, fixated on getting out of the hospital and he wasn't going to let his appearance stand in the way. It just didn't seem that important to him. He had already overcome so much. His heart was beating. His mind and his legs were working. He was *living*. He had Emily at his side and his future in front of him. And that really was the most important point. Matt Miller wasn't blind. He wasn't obtuse. He had always been very good on picking up when Emily was upset, when things weren't going right for her. He knew and Emily freely admitted she was never any good at hiding how she felt. And from the very first moment he regained consciousness, Matt was tuned into how Emily was acting around him, what signals she was sending. And there was never even a glimmer of doubt, or hesitancy, or frost. And that explains much of the reason why he'd never even thought much about his face, or concerned himself with his smile before that day, that moment. He could tell by Emily's actions and behavior that it wasn't that important to her. And when he asked his mother and Emily about his smile, that first time, he was completely tuned into her reaction, and she never expressed anything even close to mixed feelings. It was a wonderfully liberating, powerful feeling to know that the woman you loved didn't mind how you looked, that she loved you anyway. But if she had said or even hinted that Matt should think about repairing his face, or that she really wished he'd had a better smile, this likely would have created a completely different mindset for Matt. He likely would have sunk into a tailspin, and aggressively pursued surgery to restore his nerves, or reconstruct his smile. But there was never any of that. And if Matt's own mother sensed momentary fear in him, he had no recollection of it. Emily's unwavering support had made him shockingly unselfconscious, to the point where he didn't even bother to take a good long look at his face until three weeks after the accident. And when he did look, he honestly didn't think his face looked that bad. And deep down he felt it would come back.

Now, if Matt never doubted that Emily would always be with him, this could not be said for everyone.

Since the time it became clear that Matt would live, friends and even family wondered what would happen with the relationship between Matt and Emily. To put it in the kindest terms, maybe it was not so much that they wondered if she would leave, but they marveled at how she had stayed. Mark Bernardino, there day after day, played it over in his mind: Here was a beautiful girl, with a sharp intellect, and dreams of her own of becoming a doctor. And there was Matt, who potentially now was going to be permanently disfigured. This was not what she signed on for. Bernardino in the back of his mind wondered and worried what would happen, but he spoke of it only to his wife, Terry. "I kept coming home and saying, `I'm amazed that she comes every day,'" he said. "One morning I came really early and Emily was there. I said, `What the hell are you doing here?' she said, `Shhhhh! I slept here. But don't tell the Millers."

Nancy Miller saw Emily up close, and with a mother's eye, and in her eyes so far Emily had never wavered, never showed anything but love and commitment. Nancy never discussed with Emily the possibility that Matt was going to look different, maybe very different. Nancy was a positive, hopeful person, but she was also a realist. Emily was a beautiful girl. She would have many men interested in her. Nancy never had any reason to suspect that Emily and Matt's relationship might deteriorate, but she knew it was a possibility, and beyond her control. If it happened, she thought to herself, as painful and difficult as it would be, Matt would get through it. They would all get through it. But Nancy never saw a crack.

Emily never believed, not for a moment, that anything had changed between her and Matt. She frankly would have been shocked to know that people even considered it. The closest anyone came actually to raising this subject in front of her was Matt's grandfather, who, during a visit to the hospital that second week, said to Emily with the directness of an 80-year-old man: "You know his face will never look the same."

"I just want my Matt back," she told him.

After three years of dating, physical appearance was such a small part of everything she loved about Matt. And it wasn't like something was taken away. She believed he still looked beautiful, and she knew there were many other beautiful parts of him. This is how she felt. But it had been just three weeks since the accident. Time would tell.

• • •

The window of opportunity on exploring Matt's facial nerves was closing. But that Saturday afternoon, in his home away from home, Six East, Matt was adamant. He wanted no more surgery of any kind. He wanted to get out of the hospital. He wanted to believe his facial nerves would come back. He and Emily had long discussions about it, and Emily was fine with whatever Matt decided. She figured that if he could live with his face, so could she.

Doctors, too, were reluctant to do surgery, and would push for it only if they were certain or close to certain, that the nerve was truly severed. Finally, after several delays because of a broken machine, they conducted an ENOG test that Monday, the 24th, to see if they could measure any electrical current in Matt's facial nerves. Nancy's note in her journal that day revealed all one needed to know: "Matt's facial nerve tested – no response on left side."

Being able to move our faces is so much a part of who we are, how we communicate, express ourselves. What is most precious is what doctors call "spontaneous animation" – how we smile when we're laughing, or when tickled, or how our faces light up when surprised by wonderful news. These are all expressions we make on our faces without thinking. When the facial nerves die, this spontaneity is lost. Doctors like Park have many surgical tricks that can help someone whose facial nerves have died. Park can teach a patient how to smile voluntarily, but never spontaneously, never naturally.

The next day, Tuesday the 25th – two days before Thanksgiving – they were going to try one more test – an EMG, or electromyogram. Nancy knew this test involved sticking Matt with little needles, which would be sparked with electrical current in an effort to see if the nerves were working. She thought there might be some bleeding from the needles. But she also knew Matt just had to have this test. In her mind, they just had to know if doctors could find some life in those facial nerves. This was the last possible test. She also knew Matt was now on heavy blood thinners after the stent, and she feared that if the doctors and technicians conducting the test – not his normal doctors – knew about the blood thinners they might somehow refuse to administer the test. Nancy had been around the hospital long enough now to know how things worked. Cancellation was a real possibility. So Nancy told Matt, "We're not saying anything because if you bleed, too bad. We need this test. We need this information."

Park described the EMG this way: Imagine a completely dark room. The facial nerve is an electrical cord. And the facial muscle is a light bulb. The idea was to plug in the cord, run current through it, and see if the bulb lights up. In other words, with an electrical stimulus, would the facial muscle move and function?

For the test, Nancy and Matt went to the basement of another building in the hospital. Emily by this point had already said goodbye, and gone home to be with her own family for Thanksgiving. They needed her. When doctors conducted the EMG on Matt, when they ran current through that damaged nerve, the bulb did not light up that dark room. But there was the dimmest, faintest, most remote glow, a glow too weak for the naked eye to see, only powerful enough for a machine to pick up, but a glow nonetheless. The EMG showed there was life.

This faint glow and trace of conductivity was by no means a guarantee that the nerves would ever regenerate enough to make the bulb glow, to give Matt function – many times that simply doesn't happen. Park and Christophel had seen it before. There would be conductivity. The nerve should work. But it never did. In truth, a nerve need not come back all the way. Even 40 percent was enough for the face to work. And the bottom four channels of the nerve are all interwoven. They crisscross like a weed's root system, and if one were out the others could pick up the slack. So every branch didn't even need to come back to life, just some of them.

But the important thing now with Matt was that there was hope. "I'm seeing a little bit here," the doctor running the test told Nancy. "By the mouth. You should get some function back. Leave it alone." Nancy Miller didn't usually let herself get emotional, but this time she did. She just couldn't contain herself with joy – her own facial muscles were now textbook examples of spontaneous animation. She was thrilled and relieved and so grateful. She hugged her son. She thanked the doctors so. When she met with Park later that day, a normally very serious man, and he reviewed the results of the test with her and Matt, she swore he broke into a big smile as well. This was great news and a relief. Nancy wasn't so sure Matt or anyone in the family could have endured one more surgery at that time. "Matt's been battling but he's wearing down," Mike Miller had e-mailed Brennan that morning before the test. "Just don't know about asking him to go through yet another round of surgery at this time." They had all hit the limit of their own endurance – and mercifully, gratefully, they would not be pushed beyond it.

They all really needed some time out of the hospital, and maybe Matt had been right all along, maybe there was still some faint, slight chance that they could get out of there by Thanksgiving.

• • •

Through it all, Matt was sucking down his calories, determined to leave. And Nancy was recording every day: November 13, 750 calories; November 14, 1700; November 15, 1800.

On Tuesday, the 24th, he consumed 3,140 calories!

Nancy broke it down in her log:

6:30 a.m. 250 calories – Boost Breeze
7:00 a.m. 280 calories – Carnation mix (130 cal.) plus 8 oz milk (150 cal)
10:00 a.m 250 calories – Boost Breeze
10:30 a.m. 250 calories – Boost high protein drink
1:30 p.m. 280 calories – Carnation mix (130 cal.) plus 8 oz milk (150 cal)

4:00 p.m. 1,000 calories – Ben & Jerry's milkshake w/pb ice cream +
whole milk
5:30 p.m. 250 calories – Boost Breeze
8:30 p.m. 280 calories – Carnation mix with milk
11:30 p.m. 300 calories – yogurt milkshake

The nutritionist in her 19 years as a professional had never seen anything
like it, and wouldn't have believed it, if she hadn't seen it. And if Matt could
get home, and into a kitchen, with access to a blender, he told her, he could
mix together so many things, with so many more calories. He'd been reading
all about it on line, honestly dreaming about all the foods he could blend!
Matt had never reached 4,000 calories, but he'd come so much closer than
Kelly O'Donnell, the nutritionist, thought humanly possible. And on that
Tuesday, the 24th, out came the naso-gastric feeding tube. Matt Miller was
feeding tube free. No more tube clipped to his nose. His survival would now
depend entirely on whatever he could suck through a straw.

So that, coupled with the decision to forego the facial surgery, cleared
the way for discharge. Everyone's mood soared. Matt couldn't go home to
Pennsylvania, but the Millers owned a condo at the Wintergreen ski resort,
and Nancy and the doctors agreed that she and Matt could go there, and be
close enough to his doctors and the UVA hospital if trouble arose. They could
do many of the follow up appointments and tests over the next month or two
on an outpatient basis.

That same Monday afternoon, Larry Sabato called Matt for the first
time. Sabato, perhaps the most famous professor at Virginia, and a fixture in
national political circles, had been an undergraduate at the same time as Mike
and Nancy Miller. In fact, Mike Miller and Larry Sabato were in the same
government honors program together, two of just six students in the whole
program. Larry had gone on to become president of the Student Council his
fourth year, and Mike Miller had become president of the College of Arts and
Sciences and chairman of the Honor Committee. They had remained friends
all their lives, and when the Miller boys went to Virginia, they got to know
Professor Sabato, who held an endowed chair and lived in Pavilion IV on the

Lawn, the University's famous central green designed by Jefferson. Larry had spoken with Mike Miller several times since Matt's accident, but this had been an insanely busy time for Sabato. Not only was Barack Obama elected as the first African American president in American history, but on election day Sabato's widowed mother fell and broke her hip in Norfolk, Virginia. Sabato was an only child, never married, and extremely close to his mother. So while Mike had kept him up to date, and taken comfort in his phone calls, Sabato hadn't had time to visit Matt. He'd been spending plenty of time in hospitals, but with his mother. That afternoon, he called Matt, and they had what Sabato liked to describe as a long and pleasant monologue – Sabato talked and Matt listened, grunting a few times as well. Sabato joked to Matt that he would love to wire shut the jaws of many of his students so they would actually be quiet and listen to him in class.

Several hours after the phone call, around 10:00 p.m. Matt Miller sent the following e-mail from his hospital bed:

Professor Sabato,

Thank you very much for the call and the well-wishes. I am very sorry I did not get to see you and I am excited to get back in touch when I can talk! I am also very sorry to hear about your mother and please give her my well-wishes and tell her she is in my prayers. You will be happy to hear that I signed up for your class this spring, and I signed up to take it as an audit. Please let me know if this is not allowed in the course.

Once again, thank you very much for the kind call and I hope you enjoy your Thanksgiving holiday.

Best wishes,

Matt

Sabato forwarded the e-mail to Mike Miller five minutes later, adding: "I am shocked to get this! From near-death to perfect English in 3 weeks!"

It was a mad scramble to try and get out by Thanksgiving. Nancy had to arrange for all Matt's follow up appointments over the next several weeks. She had to order medical equipment – a humidifier, for instance, to be attached to his tracheotomy tube at night – and make sure she was at the hospital when it was delivered. Matt needed several medications, and those had to be prepared, and a pharmacist would need to go over the doses with her in person, and there was delay after delay getting that done. Doctors had decided that Matt's tracheotomy would be left in his throat for at least another month, in case he needed more surgeries. Nancy had to learn how to clean out the tracheotomy tube, which regularly would get clogged with mucus. Since Matt's jaw would remain wired for another three weeks, at least, doctors also needed to give Nancy a pair of wire cutters and show her how, in case of an emergency, to cut the wiring to allow Matt to open his mouth. This would be necessary, for instance, should he choke. This was all daunting to Nancy, not to mention exhausting trying to get it all done on deadline. But she was willing to shoulder almost any burden in exchange for freedom from an institution, albeit one to which she would be eternally grateful for saving her son's life, but an institution nonetheless.

Mike Miller had gone back to work for a few days, and was going to pick up Michael, flying back from Stanford for Thanksgiving, at the Philadelphia airport. Father and son would drive down to Charlottesville together Wednesday afternoon. This was a horrible time to travel but all the Millers had learned not to sweat the small stuff. Mike and Michael arrived at the hospital Wednesday evening to find Nancy stressed, trying to take care of all the last-minute discharge issues, and Matt excited and impatient to get out. Nancy sent Michael and Mike over to the Marriott to pack up her belongings – and they did about the kind of job you'd expect from two impatient men packing up a woman's things. Mike also paid the bill, which after 24 days wasn't small.

In the hospital that evening, as word spread that Matt Miller would actually be leaving, many doctors and nurses and therapists who'd been involved in his care came by to see for themselves and say goodbye. There were many hugs and moist eyes and quite a few expressions of disbelief. Not Calland, Park, Christophel, Sheehan nor Hanks – none of them – or anyone else involved with Matt's care in the early days after his arrival, would have imagined three and a half weeks earlier that Matt Miller would be going home by Thanksgiving.

Around 9:00 p.m. on Wednesday, all the issues had finally been resolved. Calland signed the discharge papers. The pharmacist had gone over all the medications with Nancy. And a nurse rolled a wheelchair into Matt's room. Time to go.

"I'm walking out of here on my own," Matt wrote her. She tried to object. This was hospital policy. But Matt was insistent. She agreed to push the wheelchair behind him, just in case. Matt, for the first time, put on the T-shirt Bernardino had given him. *Don't give up, don't ever give up...* Mike and Nancy went to get the cars out of the garage, and Michael escorted his brother as he walked through the halls of the University of Virginia Medical Center one last time. Matt felt and appreciated the significance of leaving this hospital, which so many people thought he would never do, much less do so soon. He knew how blessed he had been, how lucky. He urged his brother, by pointing and grunting, to walk out before him, to wait outside and take a picture as Matt emerged. Michael's only camera was on his cell phone but that would have to do.

Walking into the November chill, his first time out of the hospital since arriving on AirCare 5, Matt raised a fist in triumph – or as close to a fist as he could make with his casted right hand. Being from the Philadelphia area, Matt felt this was his Rocky Balboa moment. Michael took the photo – blurry but beautiful for the mere fact of what it captured. Nancy and Mike were waiting with the car. Mike was tearing up now, and even though a frazzled and exhausted Nancy wasn't crying, her heart was as full as it could ever be with gratitude, relief and joy. This was a marvelous, beautiful, emotional moment. Mike Miller hugged his son, and told him, "This is the biggest competition you've ever won!"

Actually, Matt didn't see it that way. This wasn't the ending of a competition, but the beginning – to get his life back.

• • •

The family had made no plans for Thanksgiving, and Wintergreen's buffet on Thanksgiving Day was sold out. When Mike explained the circumstances, the resort managers packed up takeout – enough food for the four of them to last two days! The meal began with a surprise, a prayer Matt had written in the hospital, and had asked his brother to read: *Thank you, Lord, for letting us be together as a family, and for watching over us, especially during these past four weeks. Forgive us for, at times, worrying about the little things that are not important rather than what really is important. Family is important and we thank you for keeping us together as a family...Amen.*

Matt then conducted his first experiment with the blender. He blended sweet potatoes with milk and sucked down orange slop through a straw. He didn't rinse the blender, so when he mixed turkey with chicken broth, it came out orange. He slurped that down. A little blended cranberry – slurp. Then he blended mashed potatoes with milk. Finally, he blended pumpkin pie with milk and even threw in some ice cream – he wanted it a la mode. The color was indescribable but then so was the taste.

For Matthew Quinn Miller, no meal ever tasted so good.

―――

MATT AND EMILY THREE DAYS BEFORE THE BIKE ACCIDENT, HALLOWEEN 2008

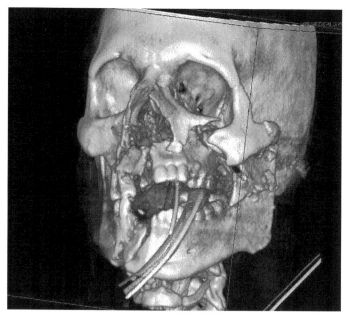

A THREE-DIMENSIONAL CT SCAN OF MATT'S FACE TAKEN TWO HOURS AFTER THE ACCIDENT.

MATT POSES WITH MARK AND MARY ANN HARRIS SIX WEEKS AFTER
DR. HARRIS SAVED HIS LIFE. MATT'S JAW IS STILL WIRED SHUT.

MATT AND EMILY POSE BEFORE GOING OUT TO DINNER,
NOT QUITE THREE MONTHS AFTER THE ACCIDENT.

MATT POSES WITH MARK BERNARDINO ON HIS FIRST DAY BACK IN THE POOL.

CHAPTER SEVEN

Late Thanksgiving afternoon, Matt's grandparents, Sidney and Wanda Miller, stopped in at Wintergreen for a short visit. They had visited once before in the hospital – Mike had given strict orders to his mother, an emotional person not unlike her son, not to cry in front of Matt when she saw him. Mike threatened to escort her right out if she did. Wanda Miller thought Matt was probably wondering why his grandmother *wasn't* crying when she saw him for the first time, but she was willing to do anything for her grandson, and if that meant holding it together, she would. Mike Miller had been careful to minimize the number of visitors to the hospital at first, because he had his hands full. And even though he loved his parents and his brothers, and had talked with them repeatedly over the last few weeks, he didn't want them coming to Thanksgiving dinner at Wintergreen, coming on that very first day Matt was out of the hospital. He just felt it would be too much for everyone. So Wanda and Sidney Miller, 81 and 82, drove from their home in Roanoke to Harrisonburg, about two hours north, and their sons Dennis and Jerry met them there. Sidney and Wanda wanted to be with family on Thanksgiving and give special thanks for Matthew's survival and recovery. Harrisonburg was a central location for all, but about the only place open was the Cracker Barrel along Interstate-81. They had a surprisingly delicious and joyous meal there, and for Wanda and Sidney, the afternoon got even better. They called Mike and asked if they could stop at Wintergreen, not too far out of their way, on the trip back to Roanoke. In this family of very determined people, Wanda and Sidney were not to be denied. The grandparents didn't stay long, but were so glad they stopped in.

Sidney Miller was the 12th of 13 children who grew up on a farm in one of the most rural and remote corners of Virginia, in the town of Jerome, still too small to make the state highway map. Sidney walked 2.5 miles to and from the one-room grade school every day. He walked only a mile to catch the bus to high school, which was 14 miles away. The local paper wrote a story about him after he graduated from high school because, according to the school officials, he never missed a day in *12 years* of school. Sidney didn't think about college. The 11 siblings before him didn't think about college, so why should he? He thought he would be content to work on the farm, like most of his family had done for generations. But that summer after graduation, on a 100-degree day in the field, walking behind a plow and the backside of a horse, it dawned on Sidney Miller this wasn't the future that he wanted. He had a friend who was going to college in Berea, Kentucky, where you didn't need to pay tuition, and could work your way through college. Sidney took a bus trip – "I think we rode forever" – and got to Berea, and they told him, "We're sorry, you're not enrolled." And he said, "I don't have any money to get home, so I'll just sit out here on the front step until you figure out a spot for me." And by nightfall, they did. And he went to Berea College for two years, working a variety of jobs at the college in lieu of tuition.

At that point, with the onset of the Korean War, most of his classmates enlisted in the armed services, and he went to enlist too. He didn't enroll in the next semester at Berea, assuming he'd be shipping out by then. But he was rejected for military service after doctors discovered that his hearing was bad. He never even knew he had a hearing problem, though now he wears hearing aids in both ears. So he moved back home and got a job in the big city of Winchester, Virginia, at Montgomery Ward, a department store, as a sales clerk. It was there he first saw Wanda, working in the men's clothing department. When Sidney came, Wanda got moved to the shoe department. It was a whole lot harder to make good commissions selling shoes than trousers but Wanda didn't hold it against Sidney. Instead, she fell in love with him. Sidney's manager seemed to have a couple of girlfriends, and left the store in the morning to be with one and again in the afternoon to be with the other. Sidney took to sales pretty well, and worked on commission, and the more his manager consorted out of the store, the more money Sidney made. Pretty soon he was making nearly $100 a week – a fortune for a young man in those days, especially one who'd come from Sidney's circumstances.

One busy Saturday the store manager came by and told him to do something, and Sidney replied that he would, as soon as he finished taking care of his customers. The boss came back a while later, very hot, and said, "Didn't I tell you to do something?" And Sidney again replied that he would, as soon as he was done waiting on his customers.

At the end of the day, Sidney went to see his store manager, and told him, "we seem to have a disagreement on how to do things, and I'll be quitting." Sidney had met the manager from the competing Leggett department store at a local lunch counter. That man would be having his breakfast at 11:00.a.m. when Sidney would be grabbing a quick lunch, and they got to know one another, and that Leggett manager asked Sidney a few times to come work for him. So Sidney quit his job and went to Leggett the next morning. But the manager from the lunch counter was on vacation, and the assistant manager told him there was no position for him. Sidney said, "Well, your man said I could have a job anytime I wanted one and I want one. Tell you what I'm going to do. I'm going to work here until he gets back. And if he doesn't want me, you don't have to pay me for this time, and I'll be on my way." The manager came back a week later and Sidney stayed on – for the next 47 years. The manager made Sidney start back in the stock room and cleaning the store, "doing all the jobs nobody else wanted to do." Sidney had to prove himself and start at the bottom, but soon he was running one department, then several departments, and eventually an entire store.

The Leggett family loved his work ethic. He worked six days a week, and went back on Sundays, when the store was closed, to do bookkeeping and ordering and advertising and whatever else he couldn't get done when the store was open. Leggett was a small, regional department store chain that always wanted to be *THE* store in smaller towns, primarily in Virginia. Sidney moved around from store to store because he realized pretty quickly that was how you got promoted, and got more money, and soon he was manager of a bigger store, then manager of several stores, until ultimately he was in charge of 30 stores.

Mike says the only day his father ever took off entirely was Christmas. He and his brothers remember only one out of town vacation their whole time growing up – to a reunion at Berea College. They drove there in the station wagon, packed with a cooler loaded with lunchmeat. Sidney regretted from the beginning that he never finished at Berea and got his degree, but once he got working, there was no turning back. He knew without a college degree he'd have to outwork everyone else at Leggett if he wanted to succeed in management. Sidney also says that he was by no means the hardest-working Miller. His mother, the 4 foot 10, 85-pound mother of 13, was still milking cows into her 80s. Sidney got where he did through hard work. His wife says proudly, "We can still outwork people who are 40 years old – both of us." And she added simply, "We raised our children to work."

After moving around like military brats, these three boys went to high school in Manassas, where their dad ran the Leggett store. Mike was always the Golden Boy, and friends in high school gave him that nickname. Mike would do the same things as other kids, pranks and foolishness, but he always knew when to quit. And even when Mike did go a little too far, teachers would never think such a great student and polite young man like Mike Miller could have done such a thing – hence the nickname Golden Boy. In elementary school one year, there was a contest to see who could read the most books. Mike came home and read all afternoon, every afternoon. He sacrificed his play time, and picked up a pound or two snacking as he read on the couch. But he won.

All the Miller boys had summer jobs because there wasn't any extra money. "Growing up," said Dennis, "there were three things instilled in you: get a good education; you will work hard; and you will save. And we're all like that. Mike's got money now, but he's still like every member of the family."

Mike was high school valedictorian. He studied hard at UVA and was accepted into the government honors program with Larry Sabato. "He was unquestionably one of the best prepared students," Sabato said. "Other people in our program would have agreed. And here's the proof. Everybody wanted to use his notes."

Yet Mike also loved to party at his fraternity, and became fraternity president, and also got elected as president of the College of Arts and Sciences, which in those days automatically meant he was chairman of the Honor Committee. This was a sobering task, because at Virginia there was only one sanction if you were convicted of lying, cheating or stealing – expulsion from the University. Mike had an incredibly busy life. "What always impressed me about him was that he had the best balance of anybody I knew," Sabato said. Mike also, of course, found time for Nancy. Nancy in many ways was the Yin to Mike's Yang. She was much more even-keeled, steady and balanced. "To the extent that he had any wild side to him," Sabato said, "she tamed that."

• • •

Nancy's great-grandfather, George Washington Richards, the Civil War surgeon, received his medical degree from the University of Virginia in 1858 and was present at many great battles.

He was at Fort Gregg, in Virginia, just days before Lee surrendered, and recounted in a long letter how 9,000 Union troops, suffering great casualties, captured the garrison defended by only 250 Confederate soldiers.

"When the Federals were forming for their final charge, I suggested to Captain Chew... to surrender, as there was no chance of ultimate success by holding out any longer. My advice was not accepted... There were so many Federals coming over the parapet in the last charge we could not shoot them all; they swarmed in and showed us no quarter...

Official records indicate 30 Confederates emerged from Fort Gregg alive.

"As for myself, I counted twenty-seven only, when giving their names to a Federal officer. I could say much more, but enough! What I have said is only in defense of the plucky men that garrisoned Fort Gregg."

Nancy's great grandfather must have had a fair amount of pluck himself. He married long after the war, and had a son, also a doctor, who settled in Roanoke. His name was Lewis George Richards, Sr.

Lewis George Richards, Jr., Nancy's father, also became a doctor. The only way he could afford UVA medical school was to join the Navy, which paid for his education. After completing his service and residency, he moved back to Roanoke to raise his family and practice medicine.

Nancy's father rotated faithfully through the free clinic for the indigent at a local hospital. Roanoke was surrounded by farms and many people just couldn't afford doctors. Her father felt it was his responsibility, everyone's responsibility, to give these farmers and others the care they needed, even if they couldn't pay. "Daddy," as Nancy called him, was a Goldwater Republican, and he liked to tell his daughter that you choose your philosophy, but you don't walk in lock step on every issue. He doubted the federal government could run any big welfare programs, but he also felt there needed to be some safety net for poor women and children and others in need, at least benefits like food stamps.

Nancy also remembers her father was often being called out at all hours for emergencies, so she knew that people from all walks of life, at any given moment, could be struck by tragedy. It was not uncommon for patients with drug addictions to show up at the door, at the dinner hour or in the evening, hoping to get pills or prescriptions. Nancy's father would tell them he couldn't give them medicines, but directed them to the free clinic. And he always prepared them a meal, or at least a sandwich, before he sent them on their way.

Nancy's father met her mother, Nelle Quinn, at a dance at UVA. Nelle had grown up in Nelson County during the Depression, the daughter of a seed salesman. Nelle's family lost most of its farm in the Depression, but was able to keep a piece. Nelle majored in botany at Randolph Macon and was planning on becoming a teacher, but instead devoted herself to raising her four children.

Nelle helped start a local swim club and Nancy was on the summer swim team. Being a doctor in Roanoke in those days was a comfortable but hardly affluent life, and Nancy was raised modestly. She always worked, through high school and college, as a receptionist in her father's office, as a store clerk, and bookkeeper at a local bank. Nancy sewed many of her own clothes.

Nancy was in the second class of women ever accepted at UVA, which went coed in 1970. More than 5,000 women had applied for just 500 spots, and about 40 percent were from out-of-state, and many from private schools. Those like Nancy from public schools became keenly aware of this distinction particularly because they had never heard of AP courses and were astonished that some students arrived already having course credits! This was not a possibility yet in Roanoke public schools of her day. Not all professors (who were mostly male) and upper class students were happy that women were being admitted into the University so at times Nancy and her classmates encountered resentment and condescension. But she and her peers generally ignored it and chalked it up to ignorance. Nancy studied hard, taking lots of history courses, but always found time to go out with friends. She dated a couple of guys casually her first two years and met Mike in the spring of her second year – his third year. She actually had a date with one of his fraternity brothers which turned into a double date with Mike and his long-time girlfriend from Mary Washington College. A few weeks later, Mike asked Nancy out for Easters weekend – the biggest party weekend of the year – and a classic beginning to a UVA relationship.

They married in Roanoke right after she graduated, and he had just completed his first year of law school. Nancy got an office job at UVA to support the two of them. Mike had to pay his own way through school. It was only after they were married that Nancy learned Mike had a poker slush fund from his undergraduate days – he apparently was quite good – and used that money to buy a car. They would usher at the UVA football games for extra money. After graduation from law school, he got a clerkship with a federal appeals court judge in Alexandria, Virginia. They settled into a lovely life in Northern Virginia. She got a masters degree in library science, then a job as a research librarian, which she loved, and then worked as an analyst at the Congressional Research Service. They waited to have children until Nancy was 32, and by then Mike was working at a big DC law firm, long hours and very successful.

• • •

When Michael was born, Nancy had a very long and difficult delivery. The baby was beset with jaundice and other complications, and doctors told Nancy she could go home, but Michael would need to stay a few more days. "The first time I saw Nancy's strength was when Michael was born," said her mother-in-law. "She looked at them, `If you think I'm going to go home and leave my baby here, you have got another thing coming. I will sleep on the floor, but I am not going home without my baby.' And she didn't go. She's a very strong woman."

Michael and Matt were raised in Alexandria until they were 8 and 6. Nancy knew how fortunate she was, able to afford being a stay-at-home mother. People swore Michael was reading at 3, but he had just memorized every word on every page of several children's books because his mother read to him so much. She took them to museums, libraries. She tried hard to create good patterns and habits both boys could model through life. The boys got half an hour of TV for Sesame Street.

"Matt and I were raised in the middle, between the Tiger Mom and how the typical American kid is raised," Michael said. "There were some high expectations, but not like sort of the extreme ones like Tiger Mom. We were never allowed a video game system, or even a computer game. It was very much expected that we would get our work done, get good grades, all those things, and then if we did that, we would have the freedom to do other things as well. But both my mom and dad were very much on top of how we were doing in school and making sure we were achieving up to their standards, which weren't ridiculous but were pretty high. If you didn't come home with an A they wanted to know why. That was definitely the expectation."

Matt felt his parents never stressed the A, only doing his best. He found it much easier, frankly, just to do enough work for the A, but somehow they could tell when that was happening. Even if he got the A, they could still tell if he should have worked harder. They never took stuff away, or grounded him or said he couldn't have friends over. It was far more subtle and effective. It was more, "Matt, we would like to see you do better," and they would say it in a way that made him feel almost guilty, *even when he'd gotten an A*. Though he didn't necessarily buy into this from the start like his brother did, the expectation was clear: You've been given an awful lot. You need to do your best.

With Mike working so much, Nancy was the one who taught her sons how to ride a bike. "We go to the park," Michael recalled, "and she makes me ride down this hill. I can't remember how many times I must have fallen, but it was quite a lot. I definitely wanted to stop. My mom is kind of half way being the Tiger Mom. 'I know you want to stop, but I know you're ready to ride this bike. You're going to keep going and learn how to ride this bike.' We were there for a while and eventually I rode the bike all the way down the hill without falling. This was her example of insisting that I could do something I didn't think I could, but it was just a matter of being hard, not impossible."

If Matt in high school was into the weight room, Michael was into the model United Nations. He had his choice of many colleges. "I think my parents didn't tell me I had to go to UVA, but it definitely wasn't a laisez faire attitude either, "Michael says. "They didn't think a 17-year-old should make this type of decision without input from his family." He was considering a liberal arts college in Connecticut, closer to where his high school girlfriend was planning to go, but when he was offered an Echols Scholarship at UVA, which provided much more academic freedom than an average student had, that convinced him to attend. Matt visited his older brother several times at UVA and knew from the beginning that's the only place he wanted to go. He wasn't valedictorian like his brother, mother or father, but he had excellent grades and boards, and got straight As his first year at Virginia.

Linda Liu met Michael halfway through their second year of college. She had been born in China, but moved to America with her parents when she was 1. Her father was pursuing a PhD in mathematics. They had raised her with an immigrant's mentality – you need to have a great education if you want to get ahead in America. One of the things Linda found most attractive about Michael was that he had a work ethic and childhood much like her own. "I remember being impressed that he was a lot more disciplined and mature than the average guy I would meet at UVA," she said. She was amazed how he would be so exhausted from swimming practice but still take the hardest classes and find the focus to study. She also remembers her first impressions of Matt – "who eats this weird food and works out five hours a day." As she got to know Matt, she saw him mature, and felt, after his accident "he really exposed his true character."

• • •

Pretty much since the days when he lay on that couch and read all those books in elementary school, Mike Miller knew he wanted to be a lawyer. He never knew why, just that it was his dream. At his Washington, D.C. law firm, he quickly became known, not surprisingly, as among the hardest workers. Mike Missal, who became a lifelong friend, first met Mike when he joined the firm in 1987 and was assigned to help Mike represent a community on Long Island that was fighting the licensing of a nuclear power plant. "I learned a tremendous amount from him about being a good lawyer, really understanding that clients are hiring you to advocate a position, and really to be able to best advocate the position you have to know your opponent's best arguments, your best arguments, everything about it. I saw up close and I learned if he's got a client and an interest, he's going to throw himself into it, sort of like what Matt had to go through to come back from what he did."

Missal, like Sabato, was amazed by Mike Miller's ability to balance his interests. He was with Mike when Nancy called to tell him she was going into labor with Matt. And his reply: "I've got to finish this brief…" Missal was shocked and told his friend: "You've got to leave right now!" Mike Miller replied, "She'll be fine." And he did finish the brief – albeit quickly – and got home in time to take her to the hospital.

A few years later, in 1991, the two Mikes were lead lawyers representing a mutual fund company that had specialized in junk bonds. The company had taken way too many risks and harmed its investors across the country.

The firm was privately owned, by two families, who state and federal governments were going after in a big way. The company was almost surely going belly up under the withering scrutiny of regulators and litigation.

Mike Miller "left the law firm and became the president of the company," Missal said, "just so we could tell regulators, 'We have an honest guy running the company. We have new management in place.' He became the face of the company from a business perspective, with full authority to make decisions." Mike Miller didn't want to do this. He loved being a lawyer. But the owners kept asking him, and threw money at him. Finally, he decided to accept the challenge largely because the company was in a death spiral and nobody thought it could be saved. "We traveled the country meeting with 36 states, meeting with government officials as to why they should allow this company to survive. Mike could say to them, 'I'm no longer an advocate, I'm a decision maker. You know who I am.' Regulators knew he had a lot of integrity. He told them he was going to make sure we fixed the problems."

Mike Miller honestly thought this would take six months. It took three years. He had given his commitment to see it through, and he did. After more than two years of spending one night a week at home, he moved his family from Alexandria to New York. The slog to save this company lasted three years, but Mike was able to turn it around, "and turned around the perception of the company," Missal said. "The company survived, and in fact is thriving today, when nobody gave them a chance."

Mike Miller always assumed he would go back to being a lawyer. But he didn't. Other opportunities came his way.

The biggest, of course, was Vanguard.

When Brennan took over as CEO, and decided he wanted to go outside Vanguard for one of his top management positions, he called a woman at an investment management firm in Boston whom he'd been trying to lure to Vanguard for years. But she had just married a school teacher and wasn't leaving Boston. She told Brennan the man he wanted was Mike Miller. She was emphatic. She had seen what Miller had done with the turn-around, seen his integrity and his work ethic, and knew the two would be a great fit. So

Brennan called, and after an hour on the phone, invited Mike Miller down for a meeting in Pennsylvania.

"I tell people all the time it's nice to be lucky," Mike Miller says. "And frankly everyone, I think, gets their lucky break at some point. But the people that recognize they're given that lucky break, and are positioned to take advantage of it, those are the people who tend to be successful."

Brennan will tell you he made up his mind after that first phone call. But Mike went down for an interview, and back for a second and was offered the job. Jack Brennan said Mike Miller has always had the courage to tell him things he didn't want to hear, when it would have been easier just to go along and agree with the boss. Brennan said Mike Miller always puts his loyalty to Vanguard above his own personal self interest. Few if any at Vanguard outwork Mike Miller, and that's saying something. Even when a foot of snow falls overnight, Mike, even at age 59, is out of bed at 5:00 a.m., shoveling his driveway until 7:00, so he can make his 8:00 a.m. meeting. He could afford a snow blower, or a snow removal service, or to sleep in and miss the meeting, but that's not who he is. Although he admits, it might be time to buy a snow blower.

It was Mike Missal who first bought a condo at Wintergreen, and who convinced Mike Miller years ago to buy one there, too. And the two friends and their families would often vacation there together. This ended up being so unbelievably fortunate, because Wintergreen was the natural place for Matt and Nancy Miller to go when they left the UVA hospital.

———

CHAPTER EIGHT

Nancy was so grateful – so relieved to get to Wintergreen. Their lives were their own. Matt could sleep through the night, and well into the morning, without interruption and which he so desperately needed. Nancy could cook for him, and do laundry, and they could take short walks outside in The FRESH AIR. And they could curl up at night, like normal Americans, and watch the John Adams miniseries, which a friend had given them on DVD. Matt could sit there on the couch with Bear, a three-foot-tall stuffed animal, which this super triathlete was never too tough to do. Matt and Michael had grown up with Bear, and Mike had driven it down to Wintergreen as a tonic for his son.

Matt and his Mom could establish a routine, which both were so eager to do. Matt dove right into his books and studies, communicating with professors, arranging schedules and deadlines for makeup tests and papers, hungry to test out his mind after the accident. He had to do daily therapy on his broken hand. Mother and son would walk together in the sun, or when it was icy and cold, on the treadmill in the Wintergreen health club. Matt was a sight, in spandex, tracheotomy in his throat, drooping face, and wired jaw. But this was the South and nobody stared and nobody intruded. People were polite. Matt was amazed at how good he felt, and he really believed he was strong enough and well enough to begin running. But his doctors would have had a heart attack and the rules were clear – no running. So Matt followed the rules technically – he set the treadmill on a steep incline of five or six, and set the pace at 4.1 or 4.2 miles an hour – a brisk walk but technically not a run.

He always loved to test himself and why should his recovery at Wintergreen by any different?

Nancy had bought a new blender and meat grinder for Thanksgiving, and Matt everyday now experimented – a pioneering artiste, avante garde – mixing and combining and pureeing and sucking down through a straw every conceivable combination of high protein, deliciously-tasting concoctions. He threw everything in that blender – chicken, steak, brownies, ham, whipped cream. He had lost 17 pounds in the hospital and Matt was determined to gain it back. Nancy ordered a Christmas wreath and small tree from L.L. Bean. They felt like they were home. Their lives were peaceful after all the noise in the hospital, all the commotion. For the first 10 days to two weeks, they didn't go anywhere, then as December came along they would drive back into Charlottesville for medical tests or academic ones. Emily was back at school, finishing her semester, and would visit on weekends, the first time bringing a cherry pie she had baked with Carrie for Matt to blend, which he did with ice cream. Nancy cleaned the tracheotomy faithfully every day. Matt had a good cough reflex, so he could push most of the mucus out himself. But the tube still required manual cleaning. Nancy would remove the small piece of tubing and clean it as instructed. She hooked up the tracheotomy to the humidifier every night when Matt slept. "The days sort of flowed," said Nancy. "We set up a rhythm."

Matt had every intention of finishing the fall semester, completing every class, making up all his work. Not only that, but he wanted to do it quickly – before the spring semester even started in January, because he intended to start and finish that semester on time, without interruption. And before he could do that, he had to finish his fall coursework. This of course was shocking to all, especially his doctors. They had never seen anyone recover so fast, never thought finishing classes so soon after brain injury would even be possible. And on top of that, his doctors thought, even if a patient could do such a thing, who would *want* to do it – so quickly after his accident, to dive into school work and challenge himself. There was a tremendous amount of work to make up. Matt had several papers to write for history and other classes, and he had physics labs to make up. Nancy just sat back and watched

Matt put this all in motion. He mapped out what needed to be done, was in constant e-mail communication with his professors, set his priorities, his make-up schedules, and immersed himself in school work at Wintergreen.

"Matt just did it," said Nancy. "It was kind of amazing."

Of all his schoolwork to make up, the most daunting task, and most controversial, was Matt's physics midterm. He wanted to take it – and soon. It clearly began to take on special significance – not just as a test of his knowledge of physics, but as a test of how well his brain was working. The one with the most reservations, who urged the most caution, was Mike. Matt was in constant e-mail contact with his father, who had left the Saturday after Thanksgiving to drive Michael back to the Philadelphia airport and to return to work himself. Mike urged Matt to take it slow, and this was evident in their e-mail exchanges.

"I love you so much," Mike e-mailed from home that Saturday evening, November 29, just two days after Thanksgiving. "You're doing just great, and I know you'll keep working hard to recover and heal. Remember, that's your number one job, no matter what it takes and how long it takes. You make your mother and I incredibly proud."

On Sunday night (four weeks to the day after his accident), Matt e-mailed his dad what he called his daily update. "We had a good visit with Emily today..." Matt wrote. "I walked on the treadmill for 30 minutes, doing 1.2 miles, some of which was on an incline. I did a few light exercises later in the afternoon also. For school, I read a chapter of physics and also did the problems for a chapter. For African History, I read two articles. I have had 4,000 calories each of the last two days and today I weighed 137 on the scale, wearing my shoes, sweatpants and t-shirt – so I figure I gained a pound...I love you very very very much Dad and I miss you and Michael already. Tonight we are watching the Bears with Bear! Love, Matt."

On Monday, Nancy drove Matt into Charlottesville for a meeting with Dr. Park, and on Tuesday morning, December 2, Matt e-mailed his father: "The facial nerve looks like it is coming back on the left side of my face below the eye. Dr. Park even thought he saw a little motion around my lower right lip, which would indicate that the nerve is surprisingly not severed – he is cautiously optimistic! The alignment of my mouth looks good still. In two weeks, as of now, he will unwire me in his clinic so I can open my mouth...." Matt also told his dad he was trying to arrange dates with all his professors for makeup exams and papers.

Mike responded, "We'll keep our fingers crossed about the facial nerve... Very important is the alignment of the mouth and jaws, so you have to be sure to keep things as still as you can so that the alignment can continue to heal – no talking, and please watch that treadmill – you don't want to jostle the face."

Then Mike added in all bold: **"Matt, when you meet with these professors, please be cautious in what you're committing to do and get as much time and as much flexibility as you can...don't commit to something that will end up putting you in a bind. Your first and most important job is healing and recovering, so please take it easy. Your professors will understand..."**

Later that afternoon, after more e-mails with professors, Matt wrote his dad again. "Here is my plan ..." He outlined a schedule of making up history papers and physics labs, using Emily as his lab partner. As for his physics test, Matt wrote, "I think I can take the second midterm as early as this coming Monday. I really want to focus on completing physics as my main priority. Let me know what you think of this."

And minutes later, his father did: "Matt – Here are my thoughts. I think you're going pretty fast here. Taking the physics midterm as early as this Monday is a stretch. Why not give yourself a bit more time? You need to study and see what you'll be able to comprehend and remember. **This will be your first 'test' of what you're capable of studying and remembering since the accident. So it will tell us a lot about things.**"

And a few hours later, Matt replied to his father: "Dad, I know you want me to be safe and I am being safe. I am telling you though that I have a full week to study for physics even if I take it this coming Monday. I have looked over the material one time, and now I am reviewing it over and over again. My energy level is really good and improving every day. Plus, for the physics final, I'm going to have to learn four more new chapters as well as review all the previous material from the semester. I would like to have as much time as possible between the second midterm and the final...."

And that evening, Matt sent his father one more e-mail, his daily update: "I had the best workout I've had yet...I read a lot of African History today and did the problems for 2/3 of a chapter of physics. I am still eating a ton and staying hungry. Also I am not getting excited yet and neither should you, but my right lower lip is moving as well as the right side of my chin, indicating that the right lower nerve which we thought for sure was shot might not be. That would simply be gravy as I have been blessed already in the amount I have recovered. I miss you very much and I'm excited to see you on Friday. My appointment is at 3:30..."

That appointment on Friday would be with Dr. Calland, the trauma surgeon overseeing all of Matt's care. This was a final examination and discharge appointment and Mike Miller wanted to ask Dr. Calland his opinion of Matt taking the physics exam so soon after brain injury. Mike was coming down for the weekend and would arrive in time for the meeting with Calland.

At the meeting, Mike expressed his concerns and asked Calland whether he thought it was wise for Matt to take the physics exam. Calland didn't pretend to understand Matt's motivations, or how strongly he was driven. He wouldn't predict how well Matt would do. All he knew for certain was that just about four weeks earlier Matt had a Licox probe in his brain and was in a coma. "By definition," Calland told the Millers, "there's no way Matt can have 100 percent of his mental capacity back." Calland told the family that takes at least six months to a year after brain injury. "My gut's telling me this is not a good idea," Calland said.

Matt desperately wanted to argue with the doctor, but his jaw was wired shut. Nancy, frankly, wished her husband had stayed in Philadelphia, or arrived later that evening – *after* the doctor appointment. She knew what her son was doing, what he was capable of. She'd been watching him every day. She thought he could do it. And she had another reason for encouraging him. Keep him focused on his schoolwork. Give him a goal. He was so goal oriented in his life, and without this goal – taking the physics test, getting right back into the academic swing, proving to himself that he could do it – his attention might turn to something else. Maybe he'd be looking in the mirror more, worrying more about his appearance, his future with Emily, all the things he'd lost. Who knows? But she believed that taking that physics test was the best thing for him. She felt he was capable and motivated. But it was risky – and the risk was far beyond a bad grade. What if Matt's mind wasn't where he thought it was? What if the test showed he didn't have the aptitude, the concentration, the brainpower that he had before the accident? Would a bad grade on the physics exam confirm these deficits? Would it send him into a tailspin of a different sort? This was really Mike's concern: Not only a bad grade, which Mike did worry about, because to this point Matt had a perfect 4.0 in all his science courses, but the damage to Matt's confidence, his self image. So this test was much more than a test. The stakes were huge, and Mike and Nancy understood this better than anyone.

Dr. Sheehan, the neurologist, for the record, didn't think Matt would do all that well, but knew how important it was for him to take the test, to push forward. Sheehan realized it was integral to Matt and his recovery that he did not back off or delay, so he had no problem with Matt taking the test. From a neurological point of view, taking the test couldn't hurt him.

The date for the physics test was set for December 11 – a Thursday. The physics professor, Hung Q. Pham, first heard about Matt's accident from Emily, who was also in the class. He had been teaching for nearly 30 years at UVA, since 1982, and he liked the premed students. They were a dedicated, earnest, hardworking crew, who genuinely wanted to learn and master the subject. He was impressed with them as a group, for their intelligence and work ethic in general, and their commitment to learning, and he frankly wished more of them would consider becoming physics majors and professional physicists. Matt was one of 180 students in his lecture class, and he frankly wouldn't have known Matt from Adam prior to the accident. But Pham will never forget the day Matt showed up in his office on the third floor of Gilmer Hall, the physics building, to take the make-up midterm. He was shocked. Matt's face was a disaster — the whole left side was fallen and didn't seem to work. Matt's jaw was wired shut and the student could only write notes, gesture, and grunt. He had a tracheotomy tube in his throat.

Pham thought to himself: *How could this young man possibly take my physics test?* Pham was nothing but kind and respectful to Matt, and never revealed his own disconcerting reaction. Pham offered to let Matt have extra time, a courtesy others in the class had received for assorted reasons and Pham felt it was appropriate in this case, but Matt declined. The one hour and 15 minutes allotted normally would be fine, Matt assured him. Pham had no idea of the significance of this test to Matt or his family – the opposition by his father, the insistence by Matt, the reservations by Dr. Calland, the motivations of his mother. Pham just knew that the class average on this test was 13 out of 20, that this was a hard test measuring mechanics, light, heat and waves. It tested not only students' level of proficiency in solving problems, but their ability to grasp concepts, to discern which problems required which concepts. Pham knew Matt's brain had been harmed in the accident, and the impact on Matt's face was evident. The professor thought to himself there is no way this young man could successfully take this physics test. But Matt took it. The test itself was multiple choice. Pham would have preferred not to do multiple choice, but with so many students in the class, that was the only manageable way, making it easy to grade. Pham thought Matt was a nice young man, but he didn't have high expectations.

Here were a couple problems from the test:

7) A solid disk is released from rest and rolls without slipping down an inclined plane that makes an angle of 25.0° with the horizontal. What is the speed of the disk after it has rolled 3.00 m, measured along the plane? (Moment of inertia of a solid disk of mass M and radius R is 1/2(MR2))

A) 5.71 m/s B) 2.04 m/s C) 3.53 m/s D) 4.07 m/s E) 6.29 m/s

16) A 16.2-g bullet with an initial speed of 870 m/s embeds itself in a 40.0-kg block, which is attached to a horizontal spring with a force constant of 1010 N/m. What is the maximum compression of the spring?

A) 7.01 cm B) 5.57 cm C) 6.34 cm D) 3.42 cm E) 1.26 cm

When Pham graded the test, he couldn't believe his own eyes. This was truly shocking to him. Matt got 19 out of 20 problems right, a 95 – only three people in the class of 180 did as well. And the class average had been a 65. Matt got both of the above problems correct. "For him to do that well after that accident blew my mind," Pham said.

After taking the midterm that morning, Matt and his mother returned to Wintergreen – stopping for a Ben & Jerry's peanut butter shake – and back at the condo Matt kept checking his e-mail about every 30 minutes, his mother said, hoping his professor would e-mail him his grade. He didn't have to wait long. By late afternoon, Matt received this e-mail from his professor:

"Matt, your 2nd midterm grade is 19/20. Congratulations, P.Q. Hung."

Pham did not keep Matt's actual exam, so he could not remember which problem Matt got wrong.

Matt forwarded that e-mail to his father a few moments later, adding this note on top: "Dad, Here it is. 95...not too bad! Love, Matt"

And his father replied: "**I am so proud of you.** Would have been no matter what the grade. Just the fact that you have the courage and determination to study for and take that test speaks volumes about you. To get a 95 is beyond belief."

That evening, Mike Miller sent an e-mail to Bernardino, telling him the results of Matt's physics exam. Bernardino understood what was at stake. "What a roller coaster ride it's been since November 2," Mike wrote. "Mark, I think you know how we all feel about you, and how grateful we are for everything you have done for us. You were the glue that held our family together."

Bernardino wrote back the next day, "Mike, Matt passed for me what was the biggest test of all yesterday. Just knowing that he is at full mental capacity is incredible!! We all know now, that without a shadow of a doubt, he will enjoy the fullest recovery possible and that he will be able to live his dreams!! I have tears in my eyes saying that!"

Sabato, hearing the news, also sent Matt a note congratulating him, assuring him that Santa would be good to him this year, and Matt replied, "Dr. Sabato, I am feeling unbelievably well and I am extremely blessed to feel so strong this quickly! You can write Santa and tell him I do not need anything at all because I have more than I deserve already – great family, great girlfriend, great friends and great physical health! The physics midterm grade was great, but to me the most important thing was it let me know my mind is where it was pre-accident. I have been extremely blessed to still have a strong functioning brain..."

When Dr. Calland heard the result of the physics midterm, he was beside himself. "Surviving brain injury," said Calland, "getting out of the hospital rapidly, that's one thing. But actually learning physics, autodidacting physics, while recovering from brain injury? That's amazing. The rest of it is pretty exceptional, but that part dumbfounds me."

• • •

Mike Miller was visiting at Wintergreen again that weekend, and following Matt's physics test, hearing there was some life in his facial nerves, everyone was feeling pretty good. Mike made a suggestion: "Let's go meet Mark and Mary Ann Harris and thank them in person."

"I'm in," said Nancy.

"I want to go," wrote Matt.

So Mike called ahead and the three Millers drove to the doctor's home in Charlottesville. Mark Harris stood on his front walk. Seeing Matt get out of the car and approach, the tears just flowed down his face. To see this young man, who he was sure was going to die on the mountain, or die within the hour, striding up his front walk was immensely moving for the doctor. And then to be embraced by him, wrapped in a hug of gratitude, this was so utterly satisfying and rewarding and unexpected and wonderful – one of the greatest moments in Mark Harris's life. "It's like seeing someone you love come back from the dead," Mark Harris said. "There he was. He was walking."

At the time of the accident, Mark Harris thought of his actions as 45 minutes of medical assistance, of doing his duty. He expected the boy to die. But even if Matt survived, Harris figured he'd hear that the boy was going to make it, which he did from colleagues at UVA. "We didn't expect to hear much else," said Harris. "We hoped he'd do well." Mark never expected a phone call from Mike Miller thanking him, much less to see this strong healthy young man walking up to his front door. "We certainly didn't expect this would be anything other than a single intersect," said Harris. Because he was an anesthesiologist, the gesture by the Millers to come and thank him and Mary Ann in person was even more affecting. Gratitude is something anesthesiologists in particular almost never see. "As an anesthesiologist, we don't really see the patient," Mark explained. "Almost nobody ever comes to us in our field to express that kind of appreciation and love. We just recede into the background. You expect the surgeon to get a lot of credit, and the other principal physicians who have a relationship with the patient. And that's it."

Not this time.

Matt had been forbidden by Park and Christophel from speaking. He was told that talking, or trying to talk through a wired jaw, could damage the alignment, cause the bones to set improperly, create immense problems. Matt was about the most motivated patient alive, determined to follow his doctors' orders to allow for the maximum healing. But there, meeting Dr. Harris, hugging him, Matt felt the moment required more than a grunt, more than any written note, more even than a hug. After the hug he looked at the doctor and spoke, as best he could through his wired jaw: "Thank you."

Through his own tears, after stepping back from the embrace, and taking a long look at Matt, Dr. Harris replied, "I'm having a real hard time believing what I'm seeing."

The Millers were invited in and soon the Harrises were recounting every detail from that November morning. Matt peppered the Harrises with notes, questions. At one point, the 60-year-old doctor got down on the floor, lying on his back, arms and feet clenched and extended, showing the position in which he'd found Matt, indicating substantial brain trauma and questionable survival.

Harris got back on the floor, moments later, demonstrating the wrestling-style scissors hold in which he used his own legs to keep Matt from jumping up and running away. Mary Ann told Nancy how she had wanted to go to the hospital that afternoon, and comfort her, but felt she would only have been intruding. Nancy pulled the wirecutters from her purse, and said she never went anywhere without them, and it was an amusing moment – the preposterousness of it all, really – that had them all laughing. They laughed even more than they cried. It was a wonderful bonding moment, one that would cement these two families forever, or at least what they all felt like would be forever.

As Matt listened to Dr. Harris recount the fateful morning in such detail, he knew the doctor was describing him, talking about him, telling the absolute truth, but Matt just could not summon any mental image. This had happened six weeks ago in his own life, but he couldn't picture it – which, frankly, was fine with him. Matt's appreciation for what Dr. Harris did was in no way diminished by the fact that he couldn't remember any of it. He felt a swelling gratitude to this man, and he could see how powerful this connection was between the two families.

What struck Mary Ann was not only Matt's physical recovery, but his emotional one. She didn't know Matt before the accident, obviously, but to see him in her family room, so positive, so determined, so grateful and full of joy, to read his notes about Emily and his school work, and his plans, she found this just as amazing, maybe even more amazing than his survival. When she was working as a social worker, she focused on at-risk children and their families. And one of the things she always looked for in kids was their resiliency. How strong could they be? How well could they survive the things they were facing? And with Matt, there was no question about his resiliency, his strength. She knew just how rare it was, and just how much it mattered.

The visit lasted over two hours. As the Millers got up to leave, Matt posed for a picture with Mark and Mary Ann. Their smiles were so broad, so full of joy, they made Matt's tracheotomy collar and facial deformities seem almost unnoticeable. As he left, Matt tapped his heart, and pointed to the doctor, one last gesture of appreciation. And as Matt walked away, Dr. Harris knew right then, that the image that would remain vivid in his memory for years to come, and maybe for as long as he lived, was not cradling a dying boy on the Blue Ridge Parkway, but seeing the same boy, so full of life and gratitude, walking six weeks later up his front walk.

———

CHAPTER NINE

Matt – and all the Millers – began getting endless e-mails and comments from people calling what happened with Matt a miracle. In the extreme, some claimed he was saved by God for a reason, and his life was now intended for something special. Many said he was an inspiration how he battled back, and surpassed everyone's expectations. Larry Sabato wrote him, "Matt, there are a few people in life who have a terrible ordeal – and then turn it into such a positive experience that they lift up others spirits just by being around them. You are one of these rare individuals. I'm very proud of you. I wish we could bottle and sell that attitude. I'd drink a bottle myself! Like most people, I have a tendency to whine about small problems that don't matter."

As Matt recovered at Wintergreen, and went back to Philadelphia for Christmas, he really began to process all this for the first time, with some perspective. What had he done? Why had he done it? What had it meant?

Matt was a little surprised that people found his recovery inspiring, because he was just doing what came naturally to him, what seemed like the only option. But if his story could inspire people, he realized this was a real privilege, and he relished this. But he wanted to be clear from the outset what about his story was inspiring, and what wasn't. As he wrote his father in an e-mail, "I do not want to be an inspiration to people because I recovered. I recovered largely because of God's blessings and great medical care. I want to be an inspiration to those who witnessed my positive attitude and sheer determination during my recovery. That is something I had control over and if I can inspire people and make a positive difference in their lives, then I consider myself lucky to be able to do so. An unfortunate part of the human experience is that it takes an accident like mine to make you realize what is truly important in life and to appreciate everything we have been given."

Matt always knew he'd been given a lot – but his accident really made him appreciate the gifts that money couldn't buy. He felt a desire over the next couple weeks to express that gratitude.

On December 19, his first night home for Christmas, he sent a note to Doctors Park and Christophel: "I just wanted to contact you to thank you again for all you have done these past seven weeks. Because of everything you have done I am sitting at home in Philadelphia right now and I will be able to spend the holidays with my family and friends…I am truly amazed at how much I look and feel like my old self which is an incredible statement to how amazing of a job you both did in the OR and since in follow up care. This will sound silly because I am only a third-year college student, but if there is every anything I can do in any way to help either of you, I will try my best to make it happen. I am completely indebted to you."

And on December 29, Matt scratched out a letter by hand, addressed to *"Mom, Dad, Michael: I was telling Emily tonight how amazing she has been these last eight weeks. The three of you have been incredible these last 8 weeks as well, and have played a huge role in saving my life and helping me recover as fast as I have. The doctors physically stabilized me, but you all healed me. While the doctors are recognized for their incredible works, please realize that you all played just as big of a part. Every word you spoke to me those first few days, every hug and kiss, every prayer you said all I promise you were vital to me healing and recovering. I may not remember those first few days, but I know how much of a difference it made having you all next to me, fighting alongside me. I owe my life to the three of you and Emily as much as I owe it to all the amazing doctors – Dr. Harris included – who operated on me. I thank God multiple times a day for blessing me with such a strong family – Emily included – who I love more than anyone loves anything in the world. I just wanted to let you know how much I appreciate your love and support, and I want you to realize just how much of a difference you make in my life. We are all more blessed than we can realize to have each other. With all the love in the world, Matt."*

It was striking to Matt how much his ordeal seemed to affect people, even people he didn't know. For instance, since his accident, he had been receiving cards and small gifts from Merrily Stilwell, a 61-year-old receptionist at Vanguard. Merrily knew Mike Miller, but she had never met Matt. Yet from the moment he was fighting for his life, she felt a connection with him because of his grit, determination. As he continued to defy everyone's expectations, she felt more connected to him. In her notes to Matt, she told him her story, what she had endured in her own life, why she felt they were kindred spirits. And Matt, after hearing her story, began to draw strength from Merrily. He realized that what he was in the process of overcoming was truly small compared with what she had overcome, and still battled every day. And Matt began to see, by this relationship that was developing between the two of them, that his recovery was not only helping himself, but nourishing Merrily as well.

Merrily Stilwell's parents divorced, and her mother died young, and Merrily bounced among four foster homes and an orphanage. Merrily Stilwell's childhood was nothing like Matt Miller's – separated even from her siblings, she had no loving family around, no one expecting and pushing her to go to college. But in that youth she found her faith and her strength, and those carried her along when she was diagnosed with multiple sclerosis at age 30. Even with her preexisting condition, Vanguard hired her as a receptionist in its executive office building in 1982, and she worked there, faithfully and gratefully, until MS got the best of her in 1998, putting her in the hospital, then a rehab hospital, then the nursing home. At one point, the therapist told her, "you're never going to walk again or work again," and that's when Merrily fired the therapist. Eventually, she got a friend just to take her home. Merrily prayed and prayed and contacted the Pink Sisters, an order of nuns in Philadelphia to whom she now has been calling and asking for prayers for decades. Merrily was determined to go back to work. Merrily would ask her friend to hang a work suit on the closet door, along with a blouse and shoes and appropriate pocketbook, so Merrily could imagine herself going to work every day. That was her motivation. She was determined to take one step, and then another, and one day get all the way to that closet door and put on those clothes. This was still only a goal, a dream, when she got a call from a human resources associate at Vanguard one day who said that Merrily's long-term disability coverage had reached a year. According to company policy her employment was now terminated and she could apply for COBRA for her insurance coverage, which, without a job, Merrily never could have afforded. It was all so official and antiseptic, as if to say thank you very much and goodbye. Merrily told the human resources woman that before she signed anything or agreed to anything she'd like to call Jack Brennan, the CEO. In 1982 when Merrily was hired, Vanguard was a small company. Brennan also had come in 1982, and so had been there at the beginning with Merrily. She didn't want to put him on the spot so she called his number at night, when she knew she'd get his voice mail, and she told him she loved Vanguard and working there meant the world to her and she desperately wanted to come back and she was determined to come back and praying and working hard and planned to come back and wasn't there some way he could keep her job for her? Jack Brennan didn't call her back so a week later Merrily called the human resources lady again, and was told that a courier was going to bring work to Merrily's house every Monday and pick it up every Friday. Merrily said it was embarrassing what kind of work it was – writing thank you notes and letters about charity events. But she was grateful for it and it kept her employed. Even more amazing, she received a note in the mail from Jack Brennan. Hand written in green ink, his trademark color being a Dartmouth alum, was this: "Merrily, Of course your position will be here for you when you return! Let's hope that day is very soon. All the best, Jack." This act of kindness by Jack Brennan fueled her desire even more. And that, along with her faith in the Lord, and the prayers of the Pink Sisters, helped her return to that reception desk and that job after two years. She was walking and work-ing again and to this day carries that note from Jack Brennan around in her wallet. And Matt Miller was frankly honored and humbled to think that Merrily Stilwell saw the same qualities in him that she saw in herself.

Merrily had made the butterfly her earthly symbol, to her a symbol of renewal, and over those Christmas holidays she had given Mike Miller a gift for Matt, a ceramic butterfly with the inscription, "With a little bit of faith, big miracles can happen." And on New Years Eve, as he prepared to drive back to Virginia in the morning with his mother, Matt wrote Merrily that he was bringing the butterfly with him, and "there is a hook in the ceiling above my bed where the butterfly will hang and watch over me and remind me how blessed I am."

They began regular correspondence that would last, in fact, to the present. She encouraged Matt from the beginning to share his story: "People who are faced with major challenges need to know that there is hope and that one must never, never, never, never give up hope." And he reported to her a few days later, "The last three months have provided me with enough happy visual thoughts to last a lifetime and happy thoughts occupy my mind all day, every day, as I truly have nothing in the world to complain about."

As December rolled into January and the new year, Matt was still in the heart of his recovery – working hard on his studies, writing papers and preparing for makeup exams. Just before he went home for Christmas, doctors removed the wiring from his jaw and he could speak again. The first thing he did was call Emily, and then his father, getting his assistant at work, Nancy Ruffini, just like always, as if nothing had even happened, "Hello Mrs. Ruffini, how are you? Can I speak with my father please?" His voice of course came as quite a shock to her. "Matt? MATT!" Matt loved being able to talk again, one more sign that his life was returning to normal. In the first week of January, back in Virginia, he had another series of CT scans, and doctors confirmed his brain was healing well and the stent in the carotid artery was functioning perfectly. Since it now appeared that Matt would need no more surgeries, and have no reason to be attached again to a ventilator, he removed his own tracheotomy tube on January 13 in Dr. Park's office. He just pulled it right out of his throat. He thought it would make a nice Christmas ornament the next year! Matt finished his make-up work and exams from the fall semester just in time for the spring semester to begin. He got As in physics, physics lab, African History and an A– in his Distinguished Majors history seminar, which by this point didn't really surprise any of his professors. (Emily, for the record, who finished her coursework *on time*, got all As and one A– as well!) For the spring semester, Matt agreed to take just three classes – nine credits – in part as a comfort to his parents and also because he was going to have to drive up to Philadelphia frequently for endless dental appointments as experts tried to figure out what to do about his mouth. As good as it was getting his voice back, every time he opened his mouth the world could see he had no teeth. Matt was also discovering, ever-so-slowly, that life was returning to his facial nerves – at least the ones on the lower part of his face. And every day now he looked in the mirror and puckered his lips, just to see if he had any more motion or control than the day before. Here was a sure lesson that beauty was in the eye of the beholder, because he loved what he was seeing, though nearly everyone else would have considered it a devastating sight.

On January 7, Matt went back to see Dr. Sheehan for a routine visit following the CT scans of his brain and carotid artery. Both looked good. The brain astoundingly showed little evidence of the substantial injuries of only 10 weeks earlier, and his artery wall looked strong and blood flow to the brain was normal. As Sheehan wrote in the medical record, "He has made a spectacular recovery since his head injuries." What honestly was more spectacular was that one week later, Matt resumed his routine of shadowing Dr. Hanks. One week Matt was a patient, and the next he was an aspiring doctor. The jaws of John Hanks and Ginny Simpson just about fell to the floor when Matt walked in but they were glad to have him, and acted as if this were as normal as Virginia losing another football game. Matt just picked up right where he left off. "He didn't have his teeth," said Ginny Simpson. "He still had an amazing amount of swelling. Half of his face was still not responding, and my god he was not embarrassed, upset, or angry. All he wanted to do was learn about the patients. I don't think I could have done that. And he came back. That's when I said this is a kid who really wants to make this happen. I was blown away that he came back. It was like he never left."

Matt was not uncomfortable or awkward about his appearance, but he obviously drew some looks and even questions from patients. One man in clinic asked Matt, "Did somebody hit you?" And before Matt could even think of responding, Dr. Hanks did: "You could say that." Matt choked back his laughter and smile, always determined to maintain a professional appearance in front of patients. But later on he had a good laugh.

Sheehan saw Matt across the hall shadowing Hanks and just couldn't believe it, but then, of course, he could. He couldn't think of another patient in all his years with the same degree of recovery. He had treated many UVA students before, bright, promising kids, and they'd all received the same level of care, but none had recovered this well or anywhere near this fast. Matt was lucky, for sure, but what he had was more than luck. Sheehan wished in vain that he could explain why everything with Matt had gone so successfully. He was just glad it did.

• • •

With the removal of the tracheotomy, Matt was cleared to begin serious exercise again. He needed to wait a couple weeks for the hole in his throat where the tube had been to heal. Calland gave him the okay on January 30. And the first thing he did was head over to the swimming pool. Bernardino cleared a lane and, naturally, put a stopwatch on Matt. Pushing off the wall rather than diving, just to be safe, Matt swam a 100-yard freestyle in 59 seconds. For a college swimmer, this is unremarkable. But for a young man who wasn't even sure his airway would work properly, this was a triumph.

From the moment he emerged from his coma, and those first days when he picked up a triathlon magazine in the hospital, Matt never had any doubt that he would ride his bike again, compete in triathlons again. While he was in the hospital, and for weeks after, he really didn't give it any more thought than that. It was just a given in his mind, with details to be sorted out in the future. On the Saturday after Thanksgiving, when still at Wintergreen, Matt and his father had met a National Park ranger at the entrance to Wintergreen and picked up Black Beauty. Matt noted at the time, in an e-mail to Tim Buckley, that the bike didn't appear to be too badly damaged. "I guess I took most of the blow," he wrote. Mike had driven the bike home and had given it to Buckley to get repaired. There had been no discussion within the Miller family or with Emily at that point about when and if Matt would ever ride again. This had been the one subject that still had been just too sensitive to bring up. But getting Black Beauty fixed seemed harmless enough and made sense, considering it was not an inexpensive road bike.

The first person to raise the issue of riding again – to get Matt really thinking about this – was Emily's father. Matt had gone out to dinner with Emily and her parents over the Christmas break. He couldn't of course chew anything, since he had only a few broken teeth, but he could still accompany them to the restaurant, and at least with his jaw no longer wired, sip some soup and converse at the table like a normal person. Back home, in the kitchen, Matt, Emily and her father were talking about how great things had been going, how fortunate Matt had been. Emily's dad said, "You need to really think about your actions from now on and not just how they affect you but others." Emily's dad didn't even need to mention bicycles. His reference was clear and both Matt and Emily understood his meaning.

Especially Matt.

Matt had no fear of getting back on the bike, no aversion, because he had no memory of the accident. But he would never forget the pain he had caused his parents, Michael and Emily because of his bicycle accident. He saw it on their faces every day during the early part of his hospital stay, and this was also one of his strongest motivations to heal – to ease their pain. His greatest regret, in fact, was the pain he had caused them, and truly the last thing he ever wanted to do was cause them such heartbreak again. But he also knew that he loved biking and training and he didn't want to give it up. Was there a way to keep riding? Late that night, he came up with an idea, and he ran it past his brother, who was home from Stanford for the Christmas holiday. "What if I never ride on a road that is open to cars?" Matt suggested. "What if I only ride on trails or closed roads? What if I only do triathlons where the roads are closed to cars?" Michael thought this was a good solution, a good compromise. Matt thought he could buy a trainer, an indoor stand, a cousin to a stationary bike, and he could just put Black Beauty on the trainer and ride for hours indoors. His brother told him this was a great idea, especially if he was serious about going to medical school, because he'd be so busy with school that riding on a trainer would actually be more efficient. He could just hop on in his apartment.

Naturally, Nancy, Mike and Emily were all uneasy with the idea of Matt getting back on a bike. When the Millers had gone to visit Dr. Harris, he had told them how many bicycle injuries ended up in the emergency room at his hospital, Martha Jefferson. Nancy knew how much her son loved biking, and she felt she could never ask him to stop riding altogether. It honestly never occurred to her. She didn't think that would be fair. But she was greatly relieved to hear his suggestion over the Christmas holiday, and she came back with an additional suggestion. She had been thinking about it. She had seen skiing on television and noticed the downhill racers wore full-face helmets. And she did a little checking and noted that mountain bikers did as well. Perhaps, in addition to staying off open roads, Matt could agree to always wear a full-face helmet. He might look more like a hockey goalie or alpine skier as he rode the Schuylkill Valley trail near their home, or along the bike paths of Valley Forge National Park, but this would be one additional form of protection. Matt readily agreed. He would look into buying a full-face helmet and a trainer, and when he was strong enough to resume riding, cycle only on closed roads. He also did some investigating and learned that some triathlons, even Ironman triathlons, took place on courses where the roads were closed to cars. So he was satisfied. This was a Christmas gift that all the Millers and Emily could live with.

In February, Matt also began to run again, easy at first, but slowly and gradually, a little farther, a little harder. He came back to Philadelphia in early February for a dental appointment, and stayed for the weekend. On that Sunday, he went for a run with Bill McNabb, Tim Buckley, Chris McIsaac and Colin Kelton, his cycling buddies from Vanguard. They met at Buckley's house, and ran six miles easy (Matt that afternoon had mapped the route on the computer to measure the exact distance. That was just Matt being Matt). They were all astonished to see how well he was doing, to be running with him, to see how high his spirits were. As they finished the run, Buckley disappeared into his garage, without Matt noticing. Suddenly the garage door opened and Buckley emerged with a shining, refurbished Black

Beauty. They had all chipped in to make it look like new again – even better than new, with upgrades on some of the parts. Matt's face lit up. Even with his slowly, but partially recovering facial nerve, he could reflexively display a broken smile. He loved this bike. If that might seem hard to comprehend, it shouldn't. He and that bike had been through a lot together. This was really his first bike. And since he had no memory of the accident, he had no terrifying feelings to attach to it.

"There was something magical about giving that bike back in perfect condition," said Kelton. "I think it represented the condition he was getting himself back to." For the Vanguard crew, this was a transformative moment. Giving Matt back his bike was a form of absolution for them. That was Kelton's own word. This was their way of putting the past behind them. It was cathartic and healing, with real symbolism as well as an expression of friendship. With this restored bike and restored man, they could bury for good their own guilt about the accident. They could all go forward.

And as the men cooled down, and reveled in the moment, Buckley and McIsaac began talking about the Ironman they had done the previous summer in Coeur d'Alene, Idaho, and how they wanted to do another. All three of them – Buckley, McIsaac, and Kelton – talked one day of Matt doing an Ironman with them, which of course had been his dream before the accident. And that day, that afternoon, Sunday, February, 9, 2009, Matt made a decision. He would do an Ironman. It might seem far off, almost impossible considering he had no teeth, a deformed face, hadn't even been back on a bicycle yet, and was just beginning to get back in shape. But he was going to do it. For him, the symbol of his full recovery would be completing an Ironman triathlon – 2.4 miles in the water, 112 miles on a bike, 26.2 miles on foot. He didn't know where, or when, but that was his goal. He was now sure of it.

• • •

In early February, Matt also surprised Emily and belatedly took her out for a birthday dinner. He was so pleased that he could go out on a normal date that he sent a photo of himself and Emily to Dr. Christophel and Dr. Park.

Matt still couldn't chew. He would crush the food on the roof of his mouth with his tongue. The problem was that the dozen or so remaining teeth in his mouth were all cracked and broken, and the exposed nerves had all become infected. They didn't really hurt much unless he actually touched one – then there would be a zing of agony that only people who have experienced dental pain can appreciate. He went to a Charlottesville endodontist who did eight root canals in February, over a few days, and that greatly improved Matt's life. A couple of weeks later, Mike and Nancy came down to take Emily and Matt out for his 21st birthday dinner, and Dr. Harris joined them. Matt was able to chew crabcakes, and this was a dramatic improvement. Matt was still months away from actually getting even a temporary set of false teeth as dentists were still trying to come up with a game plan.

Matt and Emily also visited Sabato one afternoon in February, and afterward, the professor just had to send a note to his old classmate, Mike Miller. He was so impressed that Michael, out at Stanford, had decided he wanted to go into public service law. And Matt had just told him he thought he'd like to go into facial reconstructive surgery one day, and do for others what Park and Christophel had done for him. As Sabato wrote, "They get it – most young people don't have it nearly as good. Instead of being self-satisfied, they want to do some good for others and share their happy fortune." Sabato also told his friend, "Hope Matt continues to improve. Whenever I see a student feeling sorry for himself, I tell him Matt's story. It works every time."

At the end of February, Matt sent a note to his history advisor, telling him he planned to write his 25-page research paper on the history of the University's department of otolaryngology – ear, nose and throat department, which includes head and neck surgery, and the domains of doctors Park and Christophel. "I decided on this topic because I have such a strong interest in medicine and especially otolaryngology, as you can say I have had some experience with that specialty!!!" He added, "My semester is off to a great start and I continue to be blessed in my recovery each and every single day. All eight root canals – I know that sounds painful but it really was not the least bit so – have been finished…My facial nerves continue to regrow and since you last saw me, I have regained a lot of motion in my face – you can really see it when I smile, which I'm doing all the time these days."

Matt Miller was a private person, and was uncomfortable at first with the attention, the praise he was getting, especially from people he didn't know. But as he wrote to Merrily in February, he was warming to the idea. "…I have been given so much all my life, and there is no better feeling than knowing you have inspired someone to live a better life with a stronger faith and more positive attitude." With that in mind, he agreed to visit the school in Northern Virginia where his uncle Dennis taught, and speak to 300 students in grades three through eight. Matt spoke in early March, just four months after his accident. He worked hard preparing for the speech, thought a lot about what he wanted to say. This was really the first time in his life he had addressed such a large group, and as with all things Matt, he took the assignment extremely seriously. Students, parents, teachers and staff were all in attendance, and for good luck he wore a new tie Merrily Stilwell had sent him for his birthday. "I am the most blessed person in the world," he began, and explained very simply his purpose there that day. "I hope that my speaking to you will inspire hope and inspire faith and an amazing attitude toward this wonderful life in each one of you." And if sharing his story could help accomplish that, "I would be more honored, more happy than any of you could possibly imagine."

He told them his story, how he'd been a swimmer but had quit and discovered cycling and triathlons, and fallen in love with them. He was honest with them about his family background and perspective on life. "Before my accident, I was a college student with everything in the world going for me. I never had to worry about money coming from a very successful family and parents who made sure that they did everything they could do to give me everything that I needed. I had amazing friends, and not only was my family very successful, we were very close and very tight-knit, with a lot of love. Like a lot of people who were in similar positions to the one I was in, I pretty much thought that I was invincible and unstoppable and nothing could happen to me …"

He told them about the accident, the anesthesiologist, the injuries. "Doctors did not know whether I'd live. Nobody knew what condition my brain would be in, whether I'd be able to go to classes and read books, whether I'd be able to walk." He told them the anecdote about Bill McNabb, Chris McIsaac and Tim Buckley coming to see him in the ICU, and how – "in a ridiculous state of mind" – he insisted he could still beat Chris on a bike. He told them how he was determined to leave the hospital by Thanksgiving and "spent the most meaningful Thanksgiving of my life with my family. For the first time in my life I was truly able to recognize all the blessings that I had been given. And for the first time in my life, I truly appreciated them all."

He told them: "I would not be alive today if I had not been wearing a helmet. It saved my life, and it very well might do the same for you." He told them, "the human body is incredibly powerful, incredibly resilient if you take care of it. You do not need to obsess over fitness or exercise like I may be guilty of sometimes. As you grow older, do be conscious of how important it is to take care of your body. Try to exercise. Try to eat healthy. Because not only will being in good physical shape save your life, like it did for me, but it will make you a more healthy person and you'll feel better, have more energy."

He told them he would always be grateful to the doctors and nurses who "treated me like family," but he added, "just as important were the prayers and support I received from hundreds if not thousands of people." He emphasized in particular the strength he drew from his family and closest friends and the importance of character. "Honesty, hard work, going out of your way for others, doing the right thing at the right time, these are what will build strong relationships with others. And these relationships will not only bring you happiness every single day but they will help save your life when you need them the most. It is not possible to exaggerate the importance of family and friends." He encouraged the students to create a vision for their lives and work tirelessly toward it. He quoted Joseph Forte Newton: "We cannot decide what happens to us, but we can decide what happens in us. How we take the raw stuff of life and make it a thing of beauty. That is the test of living." And he added again in his own words: "Never lose hope. Never lose faith, no matter how great of a climb the top of a mountain may be." In closing, he described what he'd been through as not a near-death experience, but a "life-awakening" one, "and today I'm living more than I ever lived before."

He received a long and loud standing ovation.

And then he fielded questions. The first questioner wanted to know if Matt could still beat Chris McIsaac on a bike. Matt said he had ridden with him the previous week. And he had. (Matt had been riding on the trainer in his apartment almost every day now for six weeks.) Another boy asked him what was his vision for his own life, and Matt replied he wanted to be a doctor now more than ever, to help others the same way his doctors had helped him. Did he ever think he wasn't going to bike again? Matt told them he never lost hope that he'd bike again and explained the circumstances now under which he would ride his bike – only on trails and roads closed to cars and with a full-face helmet. Had he ever spoken with the driver of the car that hit him? No. He'd had no contact. Matt said he had no idea if the driver even knew Matt had survived and recovered. "I'm sure he was terrified it wasn't going to be a happy ending," Matt said. "I do not blame the driver in any way. I can see why he might not want to reach out to me." Will you ever compete in an Ironman triathlon? "Yes. One day." He was certain of it.

A week later, Matt received a glowing letter from the head of the school. "I want you to know that, rapt as they were during your talk, our students later filled their classrooms, lunch-time conversations, and their parents' ears with all that they heard from you. In a hundred different ways you made an impact on their awareness, their philosophy, their lives."

• • •

Ken Gregory, the driver of the Porsche, had heard from Mark Harris over the last few months that Matt was doing much better, that he had made a remarkable recovery, and Ken Gregory was very happy for Matt. He was relieved and grateful, but still upset by what happened. He still hadn't spoken with anyone about the accident, not even his mother and sister. He knew it was a moment he would never forget, but he was doing his best just to tuck it away in his past. The images would still come back to him some nights, but less frequently now. Sleeping had been very hard at first. Mark Harris had asked him at some point that winter if he wanted to meet Matt, and Ken Gregory had declined. Mark would have arranged it, but Ken didn't want to stir the pot. Best just to leave it alone, and let the passage of time be his friend in this regard. The Porsche was still in his garage. He hadn't repaired it, and he couldn't explain why.

Three other things of note that spring: Chris McIsaac drove down to Charlottesville and together he and Matt ran the Charlottesville half-marathon – 13.1 miles – on April 18th. Matt finished 10th out of 436 men, one second behind McIsaac, in 1:27:28 – an average pace of 6:40 per mile. This was the most significant milestone for Matt since taking his physics midterm. That he could run this well after his accident, after really just 10 weeks of training, really built his confidence. Matt knew that day that an Ironman would be a realistic goal – it would just take some time.

A week after the half marathon, Matt did another speaking engagement. Robin Root, the nurse on the helicopter, organized an annual conference for emergency medical personnel – those working on ambulances, helicopters and in hospital ERs. Every year he looked for the perfect speaker – someone who had been rescued and could recount the experience. Robin had heard about Matt's progress from staff at UVA, that not only had he survived, but he had recovered in an amazing way. Robin tracked Matt down and wrote him a letter, asking him to speak at the conference in late April. Mike Miller and Craig Stock, another Vanguard colleague who owned a small Cessna plane, flew down for the talk at Blue Ridge Community College as a surprise. Matt told his story, and had 125 medical professionals crying on a Saturday morning. One man stood up, with tears in his eyes, and told Matt, "You're the reason I do what I do." With federal privacy laws and confidentiality issues, these medical professionals rarely get a chance to hear about the successful outcomes, to see the fruits of their labors. Robin Root was probably more amazed and moved than anyone that day. Not only did he have a hard time believing this was truly the same young man he had intubated less than six months earlier, but he couldn't help but think this young man, so articulate, so driven, so fortunate, was destined for something special.

Matt's paper for his history honors class was titled, "Otolaryngology at the University of Virginia Medical Center: A History of the Department." Not only did he receive an A, but on May 11 he was notified that the paper had won an award, the Tom and Lynda Garnett Prize, given each year for the best research paper on the history of UVA. This news gave his recovering facial nerves another chance to do some spontaneous smiling.

CHAPTER TEN

Matt finished his third year of college with straight As and came home for the summer with two main focuses: study for and take his entrance exam for medical school, and visit dentists.

In mid-June, for instance, he went to see Dr. Bruce Singer in Jenkintown, Pennsylvania, a Philadelphia suburb, to get his temporary dentures. These would be the dentures Matt would use while permanent reconstruction work on his mouth was just beginning. After Dr. Singer finished that day, Matt would actually have a set of teeth in his mouth again for the first time since the accident.

After 90 minutes of drilling, sanding, polishing, buffing, gluing and photographing, the teeth were in place and the dentist was satisfied. He handed Matt a mirror.

"Wow," Matt said, softly. He was quiet for several seconds, just taking it all in. Finally, he said, "That's a smile."

He swirled his tongue all around his mouth, experiencing a strange new sensation – teeth.

Aside from that dental appointment, the first half of the summer was dedicated to studying for the Medical College Admissions Test, or MCAT.

The medical school application process is not all that different from the undergraduate application process. Medical schools look at grades and boards, extra-curricular activities and letters of recommendation. But the first two, grades and boards, matter most. The MCAT is taken all at one time, but is broken into three parts – physical sciences, biological sciences and verbal reasoning. For many people that would translate into pain, misery and suffering.

Like many aspirants, Matt and Emily enrolled in an MCAT preparation class. For five weeks, they attended class eight hours a day, learning about the test, getting advice on how to approach it, taking practice tests. Matt and Emily would come home from class and study much of the evening. Matt remained devoted to his training. Working out energized him and helped him focus. Emily often went to yoga classes. For June and the first two weeks of July, that was pretty much their life.

They took the MCAT on July 17.

Even though they had another whole year of college to complete, Matt and Emily began applying in September, and spent the rest of the summer completing their medical school applications. The process can be long and full of anxiety. Successful applicants will get invited for interviews. These invitations could come as early as September, as late as March, or not at all.

Needless to say, competition is intense. In 2009, Emily and Matt were among 42,742 aspiring medical students who applied to medical schools for the fall of 2010. About two in five – 18,665 applicants – would be accepted and enroll in one of the nation's 130 medical schools in the fall of 2010. It was a daunting and disappointing process for many, if not most. And this didn't even take into consideration the fabulous students who decided as undergraduates – when confronted by the competition from their peers, or the difficulty of organic and physical chemistry classes – to abandon their dream before even taking the MCAT exam.

In the case of Matt and Emily, their anxiety was compounded by a commitment they had made to go to medical school together. They were determined to attend the same medical school. And if wasn't possible, they would attempt to go to medical school in the same city. Philadelphia, for instance, had four medical schools. They would just have to see how the process played out.

Matt, not surprisingly, wrote his application essay about his odyssey of the previous nine months, and what he'd discovered about himself. His ending: "I will always remember my experience and I'm certain it will make me a more empathetic caregiver. I will do everything possible to allow my patients to realize their dreams, just as my physicians and so many others did for me."

He also asked Dr. Hanks to write him a letter of recommendation. It was a general letter, to be included in all Matt's applications. After reciting some of Matt's accomplishments – 3.95 college grade point average, Dean's List for three years – Hanks also summarized Matt's accident and recovery. "This is truly a miraculous story in that virtually any other patient in this situation would have taken the semester off to recover from their injuries." Hanks also talked about how Matt had shadowed him. "He quickly became a friend of the entire surgical team. He has a mature attitude around members of the medical profession and will be an excellent physician. We noted all of this prior to his accident. The strength and courage that he demonstrated in his recuperation taught us all a lesson and we became even more impressed with Matt's inner strength, courage and personal traits."

Hanks concluded: "I have met very few people with the characteristics and potential that Matt Miller demonstrates. There is no question in my mind that he will be an outstanding physician and perform at a top academic and professional manner in medical school. I hope that your Admissions Committee has a chance to interview him and get to meet this remarkable young man. …I sincerely hope Matt stays with us here at the University of Virginia; however, I am sure he will get acceptances to many fine medical schools such as yours."

• • •

A week after Matt took the MCAT, he spent the day in the dental chair of Dr. Alan Meltzer, undergoing surgery on his lower teeth, or what was left of them. Meltzer sliced open Matt's lower gums to inspect the roots of the teeth. Seven teeth were extracted, including three that had been broken off below the gum line. Meltzer did bone grafts and gum grafts that day trying to shore up the base, preparing Matt for dental implants that would come months later. Matt opted against general anesthesia, to Meltzer's surprise, and seemed fine with valium and Novocain.

Reconstruction of Matt's mouth would be primarily a two-person job. Alan Meltzer would do the foundation – rebuilding the bone and gum, yanking out the bad teeth, putting in implants. And Bruce Singer would create the new teeth. Meltzer, whose office was in Voorhees, New Jersey, just across the river from Philadelphia, was a periodontist. Singer, in Jenkintown, Pennsylvania, a Philadelphia suburb, was a prosthedontist. There were other dentists involved along the way – doing root canals, lab work, cleanings – but these two were like the Ruth and Gehrig of the dental batting order.

Art, rather than sport, might be a better analogy. When Meltzer first looked at Matt's mangled mouth, for instance, on January 16, of 2009, just 10 weeks after the accident, he said just as Michelangelo had seen *David* in a slab of marble, he needed from the outset to see a vision of where Matt would end up. Singer used a similar analogy, only he referred to Michelangelo's *Prisoners*, a collection of sculptures with only a face, or an arm, carved from a block of marble, as if to imply these perfect figures were already inside the stone, and Michelangelo had to free them. The point being that from the very ugly beginning these two dentists needed to envision what the final recreation would look like, and explain to Matt and his parents how they were going to get there, and of course the Millers literally and figuratively had to buy in.

From the standpoint of both dentists, the level of complexity was enormous. First, they had to let the jaw and bone heal from the surgeries by Park and Christophel following the accident, just to see what they were dealing with. As Meltzer said, they had to "let the seas calm." Then Meltzer had to explore – with two long and painful dental surgeries, the first right after the MCAT – which teeth could still be used in the permanent construction; which teeth needed to be removed; and which broken teeth would remain just for a while, as foundations for temporary teeth, while all the permanent construction was being done. The whole process was expected to take almost two years. In all, Matt would need more than 40 dental appointments.

On August 17, Matt and Emily got the results of their MCATs. Both scored well above the 90th percentile. This good news helped Matt perhaps as much as the valium and Novocain the next day, August 18, when he was back in Meltzer's dental chair for the second major oral surgery, this time on his upper teeth. Meltzer cut open the gums to inspect the roots and bone support, extracted five teeth, and performed more bone and gum grafts. Many of the teeth extracted by Meltzer were the same teeth that had received root canals the previous spring. He just felt the teeth were unstable and had to go. Meltzer was trying to create a solid foundation for the dental implants that would follow.

When pulling out bad teeth, Meltzer had to be extremely careful. Applying too much pressure, or pressure in the wrong spot, could have fractured parts of the jaw repaired during the original surgery by Park and Christophel. In trying to map out where he would later put his implants – Meltzer had to work around all the titanium plates and screws. And scar tissue presented a problem for both Meltzer and Singer.

Most of the six billion people living on the planet get two sets of teeth: baby teeth and permanent teeth. Because of the advance in technology and skill of his dentists, Matt was going to get a completely new third set of teeth. If all went well, they would last a lifetime. These teeth were going to be superbly engineered, durable and beautiful. They would not be cheap. In all, the creation of Matt's third set of teeth, including root canals and lab work, probably would cost in the vicinity of six figures. The Millers had excellent insurance and resources of their own. Meltzer noted that Matt and his family were fortunate that they didn't have the added stress of wondering how to pay for all the work. "What if he was some poor kid from the mountains of West Virginia?" Meltzer said, and then answered his own question. "He would have probably ended up maybe with dentures and a couple partial plates, and some broken teeth, and, you know, something far less than this, that's for sure." Meltzer said he had a similar patient from Missouri, whose parachute didn't fully open, and she suffered equally severe facial trauma. He did her entire dental reconstruction for free. "I just felt bad for her," he said. "I don't know what would have happened if they didn't have the money," he said of the Millers, "but the bottom line is there are times when part of being a professional is stepping up and taking care of somebody."

Singer gave his take on the subject: "Most of the time if a practitioner is sophisticated enough, and I've taught this, you can change a treatment plan to cost less as long as the principles stay the same. Matt could have been restored with dentures instead of crowns but the quality of life and the quality of his life as he went through it would have been diminished."

Singer added that a reconstruction like Matt's would only be accessible for most patients if insurance companies covered most of the costs, as they did for Matt. And he believed insurers would only be willing to cover such costs after a case of extreme trauma, as in Matt's case. "I don't know if a third party (insurance company) would ever pay for this unless it was an accident," he said.

The overall cost of Matt's medical and dental care, including his 24 days at UVA hospital, was probably well into seven figures. Too many doctors, insurers, and providers were involved, Mike Miller said, for him to try and come up with an actual total. "There is no single source, other than perhaps me, that could pull everything together, involving all the various hospitals and surgeries, doctors and specialists, other medical care providers and services, medication and drugs, dental work. Certainly fair to say it's been a lot, but the breakdown of charges, amounts paid by insurance, amounts we've had to personally cover – it's been somewhat overwhelming just to try and stay up with it all."

Whatever the cost – $1 million or more – could anyone argue this was not money superbly well spent? Dr. Sheehan, who did a fellowship year in New Zealand, pointed out that in many countries of the world, most in fact, Matt never would have made it to the hospital alive, much less received the care he did once he got there. In Matt's case, the American healthcare system sparkled like the jewel that it can be.

As these two dentists worked on Matt, through that summer and fall of 2009, each marveled at Matt's attitude and spirit, just as many doctors and surgeons had before them. "If you believe in the reincarnation of souls," Meltzer said, "I would call him an old soul. He's been around before. It goes beyond his level of intelligence. It's maturity well beyond his years. I never heard him complain, whine or ask `why me?' Never."

• • •

On September 13, Matt drove to Washington, D.C. and competed in his second triathlon since the accident, known as the Nation's Triathlon. This competition was much shorter than an Ironman, but hardly a sprint. It was exactly the same distance as the triathlon event in the Olympic Games: 1.5-kilometer swim, 40-kilometer bike and 10-kilometer run. That translates to a 1-mile swim, 25-mile bike ride and 6-mile run. Matt finished 28th out of 2,488 men, first in his age group for men 24 and under. He swam in the Potomac River and biked and ran along the Rock Creek Parkway and National Mall, which were closed to cars during the race. He wore his full-face helmet on the bike ride.

When he got back to Charlottesville, he found e-mail invitations to come for medical school interviews at several schools, including Virginia and Temple. Emily had received invitations as well.

Matt's final year of college was starting out pretty well.

And so was Emily's.

And kept getting better.

By October 15, both Matt and Emily had been accepted to Temple Medical School. By Halloween, both had been accepted into UVA Medical School. Matt and Emily would have been happy to attend either one, but the process was far from over, and still not without anxiety. They needed to try and balance their individual preferences with what was best for them as a couple. What if one got into the University of Pennsylvania (Penn), and the other didn't? Would one go to Penn, and the other to Temple, both in Philadelphia? Or would one pass on Penn and both attend UVA, or the University of North Carolina? There was no point speculating or working out scenarios until they knew all their options. Matt was confident it would all work out for the best, whatever that may be.

On November 2, the first anniversary of his accident, Matt felt compelled, for reasons he didn't really understand and couldn't explain, to return for the first time to the scene of the accident. It just felt like the right thing to do. He and Emily drove up there that morning. He didn't tell his parents in advance because he thought it might upset them and he didn't want them to talk him out of it. It was a cool, drizzly, overcast morning. He and Emily were largely silent on the drive up to the Parkway. They parked right at Milepost 12.2. Nothing about the spot felt or looked familiar to Matt, any more so than any other part of the Parkway which he'd driven many times over the years. Even in the drizzle, he was struck by the beauty, the perfectly groomed landscapes, the majestic scenery. Matt was so grateful he remembered nothing of his accident, and reflected on his last actual memory of that morning – the joyous celebration at Reeds Gap. He and Emily said a prayer together, thanking the Lord for his grace and blessings. They spent about 15 minutes at the site, just reflecting privately, and then they drove back to Charlottesville.

Matt felt compelled also that day, back on the Grounds, to send notes to the doctors who had been responsible for saving his life.

To Dr. Calland: "Thank you for everything you did a year ago and allowing me to be where I am today."

Calland, who had heard about Matt's acceptance to UVA medical school, replied: "Congratulations – can't wait to have you on my service. You are an inspiration to us all."

To Dr. Park, Matt wrote: "Thank you for everything this past year." To which Park replied just as succinctly. "It has been a heck of a ride. Strong finish."

Mike Miller sent a note on November 2 to Mark and Mary Ann Harris, thanking them for saving Matt's life, noting all the blessings that followed, and saying how he'd been thinking about them much of the day. And Mark Harris replied, "Your family has all been enriched to learn how many friends stand with you and how many strangers have been touched by the events. Now we learn that Matt & Emily will attend medical school and follow their dreams. How could our prayers have been answered any better? How could one doubt the hand of God?"

On Sunday night, December 13, Matt came home after finishing his last final exam of the semester. And on Monday morning, the 14th, he was back in Dr. Meltzer's dental chair. He had 15 dental implants and three more extractions that day. Matt again refused general anesthesia, thinking the valium and Novocain would be enough, but he soon realized he had made the wrong decision. He actually felt bad for Dr. Meltzer, because having Matt awake made it much tougher on him. After five hours of dental surgery, Matt's lower face ballooned again. That evening his father remarked, "he looks a bit like he just went 15 rounds." Still, though Matt didn't want his dentist to know, he went biking the next day. Because his face was so swollen, he acknowledged, his full-face helmet "had a little trouble fitting."

• • •

Over that winter break, Matt pretty well decided that the following November, over Thanksgiving of 2010, just two years after his accident, he would compete in an Ironman Triathlon. He talked it over with his Vanguard friends – Buckley, McIsaac and Kelton. All four of them pledged to enter the Ironman in Cozumel, Mexico, on November 27, 2010. They would be like the Three Musketeers and D'Artagnan. The race seemed perfect for Matt. He would have the coming summer to prepare. And while he would be in medical school that fall, somewhere, he would minimize his absence from classes because the triathlon would be the Sunday of Thanksgiving weekend. He realized that training for a triathlon while starting his first semester of medical school might seem a challenge, perhaps even insane. But he had concluded that completing an Ironman was extremely important to him, a goal he had set for himself and was determined to reach. And the deeper he got into medical school, and residency, the harder it would be to find the time to train and complete the task. This was the goal he had set for himself. This would be for him the symbol of his full recovery from the accident. Cozumel would also be perfect because that Ironman would take place on roads that would be closed to cars.

So the foursome pledged to compete in Cozumel. They also agreed to set up a Google calendar, so they could all follow one another's progress online, see what workouts each was doing, encourage one another. Each would train by himself on a daily basis, but through the common workout calendar they could in a sense prepare together. All for one and one for all.

• • •

In early March, Matt learned that he had been rejected by Duke University Medical School, where he felt he had his best interview, and waitlisted at Columbia. And then on March 15, both he and Emily found out they had been accepted at Penn. This made their decision easy. They were going home to Philadelphia. They went out that evening to celebrate at Mellow Mushroom, their favorite pizza joint in Charlottesville on the college strip known as The Corner, and then went back to Matt's apartment and opened a bottle of champagne.

If competing in an Ironman had become one goal for Matt, one symbol of his full recovery, going to medical school had been another goal and symbol. And to be accepted at Penn, one of the best medical schools in America, was more than just a symbol, it was a turning point in his life. As happy as he was, the moment was also in a real sense bittersweet. Matt actually had a heavy heart and some difficulty letting his UVA doctors know that he'd be leaving, attending Penn instead of UVA. All of them understood and were nothing but congratulatory. Park, for instance, always knew Matt would get into a top medical school, and believed Matt would make a superb doctor – and not because of any empathy he might share with patients following the accident. Park knew Matt had a relentless determination to see something through to perfection, to do it over and over until he mastered it, never settling for less than excellence – and that attitude would make him a great surgeon. All these doctors who treated Matt had hoped one day to have him rotate through their service as a third- or fourth-year medical student. But in many ways leaving Virginia was probably the best decision for Matt. He had a fabulous relationship with his doctors. He would always be in their debt and to the University of Virginia Medical Center for saving his life. Perhaps it was best to close that chapter of his life in Virginia and tuck it away as a remarkable jewel and move on. To paraphrase Humphrey Bogart in *Casablanca*, he would always have Virginia.

Graduation that May was a felicitous affair. Mike and Nancy Miller hosted a dinner the evening before at the Ivy Inn and invited so many of those who'd been central characters in Matt's life. John Hanks and his wife, Bonnie, came, and Mark and Mary Ann Harris, and Mark Bernardino and his wife, Terry, and Larry Sabato. And they of course were all in addition to Michael and Linda and the extended Miller family, along with Emily and her family. As Sabato wrote Mike a few days before, in classsic Sabato style, "Wouldn't miss it. This is the 'miracle dinner.' "

———

CHAPTER ELEVEN

In his first semester of medical school, Matt was happier than he had ever been. He loved medical school, and so did Emily. Truth be told, she might have even loved it more than he did, if possible. About 160 fabulous students from a wide variety of backgrounds were thrown together into this intense and marvelous new world. At the White Coat ceremony on the first day, Steven Gluckman, a specialist in infectious diseases and director of the school's global medicine program, told the future physicians, "I think that we have the best job in the world... Our patients allow us to have relationships with them that are unique. They trust us. They confide in us. They literally put their lives in our hands...So try to see past the insurance forms, the pre-certifications, the increasing number of hospital rules, the potential legal threats and focus on what has fundamentally not changed: your patients, your colleagues, your trainees, and your families." Their first year would be one of discovery and memorization, where they would learn all about the magic of the human body. The University of Pennsylvania, and probably all universities, worked hard to create a bond, a unity, among these new students, a cohesiveness, since they would be studying together, eating together, learning the age-old craft of healing together for four years. Emily loved the community, the friendships, something she really never had to this degree in high school, at East Carolina, or at Virginia. She also loved living in the city. Both Matt and Emily had apartments in Center City, a few blocks from one another and a 15-minute walk from the medical school. For Emily, a great release from the studying and a special treat was to find a trendy new restaurant every few weeks and go out to eat. Matt loved it all too, but honestly, he was busier than Emily, busier than just about everyone.

As Emily said, Matt pretty much trained and studied, studied and trained, and went to class. On a typical autumn day for Matt, he was up by 5:00 a.m. and on the trainer in his apartment for at least two hours of biking. Then he would make himself eggs, toast and jelly, and prepare three peanut butter sandwiches on wheat bread to take with him as snacks, and head to his first lecture, usually biochemistry, by 8:00 a.m. Every lecture at Penn's medical school was videoed, and students didn't actually need to attend the lectures because they could watch them on their computers at any time. Many felt comfortable skipping the 8:00 a.m. lecture and catching it later. But Matt knew that he learned best by attending class, so he was always at the 8:00 a.m. biochemistry lecture. That was usually followed by an anatomy lecture, and then an hour or two in the cadaver lab, allowing a hands-on exploration of what he'd just learned in lecture. When his classmates took an hour break from lab and classes for lunch, Matt typically dashed over to the University of Pennsylvania pool for a quick 2,000-yard swim, and then back to class. Most students wore scrubs to the cadaver lab because they didn't want their clothes reeking of formaldehyde all day, and stashed their clothes and books in nearby lockers. Matt squeezed his swimming gear into the locker as well.

Matt had had an intense summer of training for his triathlon – spending up to 20 and even 30 hours a week of biking, running and swimming. His Google calendar that he kept with the Vanguard boys – McIsaac and Kelton – was impressive, and he had been more fit than any point in his life. But medical school had put a serious dent into his training, which he knew would happen, and he was down to about 13 to 15 hours a week, still a lot but on the low, low side in terms of preparation for an Ironman triathlon. But he squeezed in all the training he could manage. Matt was in bed pretty much every night by 10:30 or 11:00. The medical school threw a party for all the first year students after their first anatomy exam, as sort of a reward and opportunity to blow off steam, but Matt couldn't go. He skipped it in favor of a six-hour workout – four hours on his bike trainer, two hours running – and then went to bed. "Where's Matt?" the other students at the party asked Emily. "He's on the bike," she replied. At least Emily could keep him in the loop on all the news and gossip from parties and dinners he couldn't attend. "I'm his ambassador," she explained, "so he's not really missing much." Matt knew how fortunate he was in so many ways to have Emily in school with him. "There's no way I could do this without Emily's support," he said. She also tried her best to be playful and to surprise Matt. That's just who she was and how their relationship worked. In anatomy lecture, for instance, she asked the professor, between slides of body parts, to slip in one slide that said, "Happy Birthday, Matt Miller." Matt would never in a million years have wanted or expected such a thing, but he was a good sport and Emily loved it when the whole class sang Happy Birthday to him.

Matt didn't broadcast to everyone at Penn that he was training for a triathlon, or why. He did tell the people closest to him, such as his partners in the cadaver lab and in some of his study groups. And classmates who saw him every day couldn't help but notice his tracheotomy scar, and a few of them just asked him about it, and Matt just answered them honestly. In some cases, he told them the whole story, and explained about his pursuit of the Ironman. Many of these fellow students were amazed not only that he would want to try and do an Ironman triathlon during his first year of medical school, but that he *could*. And this was a pretty accomplished crowd. "I don't know how he does it," said Mike Abboud, 22, a partner in cadaver lab. "I'll ask, 'What did you do this morning,' and he'll say, 'I went on an 18-mile run.' And I'll say, 'Well, I slept.' "

The first year of medical school requires an immense amount of memorization. Students essentially have to learn every nerve, muscle, bone and system in the body. In the process, they learn a whole new vocabulary. For example, their anatomy professor began lecture one morning with a question from a previous year's quiz: "The extensor digitorum and the extensor digitorum brevis are innervated by the deep fibular nerve that's in the upper limb. True or False?" (False, if you really must know.) When the professor added that, "This is the last lecture of the block. At no time will I mention a new muscle," cheers rang out in the lecture hall. No new body parts to memorize!

Matt would take copious notes, writing down important facts such as: "proximal nerve lesions will have more signs and symptoms than a distal lesion." The students learned the differences among the median, ulnar and radial nerves, and that "thumb abduction is controlled by two nerves, radial and medial." There was so much to remember that the students often used mnemonics to help them. For instance, "Tom, Dick and Very Nervous Harry" was a way to remember the tendons, nerves and arteries that go through what is known as the tarsal tunnel in the lower leg.

What they learned in the classroom about anatomy was usually brought home in a much more direct and sensory way in the cadaver lab. Matt and his team learned on the cadaver of a 90-year-old woman who had died of metastatic cancer. Matt and his peers treated their cadavers with the greatest respect, which included a small ceremony at the beginning of the term in which they learned some basic facts about the person and collectively acknowledged their gratitude for such an opportunity. These future doctors were literally getting their hands on all parts of the human body for the first time. One afternoon, Matt took his scalpel and sliced vertically down the right calf, peeled away the skin, and then began his exploration of nerves, tendons, arteries and muscles. At one point he held the sciatic nerve, thick as tubing, in his hand. "Without this," he said of the cadaver lab, "it would be 10 times harder to understand what they're saying in class."

Matt, not surprisingly, was particularly excited to learn about the anatomy of the face. He discovered, however, that the lecture was actually much more enlightening and fascinating for him than the actual dissection, because in reality the nerves of the face were so thin it was often hard to find them on his cadaver. He also discovered, unexpectedly, that of all the areas he studied and learned about that first year of medical school, it was the brain that fascinated him the most. And the more he studied the brain, the more he learned in lecture, the more he realized just how lucky he had been.

• • •

On Sunday, October 10, 2010, mid-way into his first semester of medical school, Matt left his apartment at 5:30 in the morning and drove to the Jersey Shore, to Island Beach State Park, to compete in a triathlon. This was really a baby triathlon by Ironman standards, but Matt was going primarily as a dress rehearsal, a warm up. He wanted to practice his transitions, from the swim to the bike, and the bike to the run, one last time before his Ironman in Mexico over Thanksgiving. He was in excellent shape, and he was going to put a good effort into each leg of the race, but he wasn't worried about his time or place or even his performance. He was just mainly doing this as a trial run, a tune up, to get out any kinks that might arise. The Ironman was exactly seven weeks away.

In comparison, this triathlon was truly a sprint – a quarter-mile swim in the ocean, a ten-mile bike ride, and a three-mile run. Matt, like nearly everyone that morning, wore a wet suit, because the water temperature was in the 60s and just too cold for most people. In Cozumel, the swim would be in the much, much warmer Caribbean Sea, where the water temperature was expected to be in the mid-80s, and swimmers would be more concerned about being too warm than too cold. Matt also wore a special triathlon goggle, which was wider than a typical Speedo racing goggle used in a swimming pool. This was in part because it increased his visibility in the ocean, but also because one of the lingering effects of Matt's accident and nerve damage was that a conventional Speedo goggle no longer worked for him. It would always leak around his left eye. Matt had arrived early at the triathlon site and set up his bike in the transition area, with full-face helmet, shoes, water bottles and energy bars, everything just so. He was calm and confident as the race was about to begin, and was in the first wave of swimmers to plunge into the ocean. He swam well and was the first of 273 contestants that morning to emerge from the water and run up the beach toward the parking lot and transition area. Matt rode smoothly and ran comfortably and finished 5th overall, with a time of 54 minutes and 54 seconds. The transitions had gone well for him and he felt good. He hadn't pushed himself too hard on any leg. This was just another workout for him. He had accomplished his mission. He was in good spirits and talkative on the drive back to Philly.

The second anniversary of his accident would be in just three weeks. There was so much going on in his life that he didn't expect to mark the day in any particular way. He had resolved not to let that accident be the defining event in his life, and he'd moved on to a new phase, medical school. At the same time, however, he said that not a day had gone by that he didn't think about this accident, and he didn't think a day ever would. This wasn't a bad thing or even a good thing. It's just how it was. Somebody might ask a question about his tracheotomy scar. Or his goggle might leak. Or his jaw might be stiff for a moment. Or he'd put on his glasses in the morning, a reminder of his accident, because ever since he could no longer wear a contact lens in his left eye. Or he might get a card from Merrily Stilwell, or an e-mail from Mark or Mary Ann Harris. Or sometimes, when snacking on a bagel, the left side of his face would start to sweat. This was known as Freyes syndrome and was not uncommon for someone who had undergone extensive facial trauma. One of his facial nerves, in the healing process, had not rewired exactly right, and somehow chewing triggered the parotid gland, a sweat gland. Doctors had some ideas how to solve that problem, and one of them included a shot of Botox every six months, but Matt would deal with that minor issue after his Ironman. Overall, amazingly, nearly two years after his accident, his life was incredibly normal and full.

While he felt God's blessings every day, and would always know how lucky he'd been, he said he felt no survivor's guilt, no special burden to accomplish something extraordinary with his life. Well before his accident Matt knew he'd been one of the most fortunate people on the planet, and had been determined to make the most of his gifts and opportunities. After the accident, Matt was more determined than ever. But rather than feeling any special burden, in fact, he felt a certain liberty, or perspective. He was sure he was finding more joy in every day, and was less likely to get upset when things didn't go his way. In a real way his accident had been a great gift. He felt he had a much better appreciation for what was important in life, and what wasn't.

He was excited about the Ironman, and what it represented for him, and the challenge it presented, but he had also learned that what he really loved even more than competition was training. If he loved training before the accident, he loved it so very much more *because* of the accident. Having come so close to death, and to physical and mental disability, just the mere fact that he still could feel the pull of his arms through the water, the pumping of his legs on the bike, the rhythm of his stride as he ran made him treasure these physical actions all the more. The diversity of the three forms of exercise only added to his overall enjoyment of them. In medical school, and in training for this Ironman, Matt Miller was pushing his mind and body to their limits, and he never felt more alive, more full of hope about the future. He even splurged and ate a donut on the ride home from the Jersey Shore.

• • •

On that drive home, Matt turned the conversation to another former University of Virginia swimmer, Fran Crippen, who also happened to be from the Philadelphia area. Fran was 26, four years older than Matt, and had graduated from Virginia before Matt arrived there. Matt had only met him twice. But Fran was a legend in Virginia swimming, and Matt was blown away by what Fran had accomplished in college and by what he was attempting to do now: win the 2012 Olympic gold medal in the 10,000-meter (six-mile) open water swim. Matt's point that morning was this: Many people had given him an awful lot of credit for his resiliency and determination, for his optimism and drive. But in terms of leadership, inspiration and work ethic, Matt felt he paled in comparison with Fran Crippen. *That guy* was an inspiration, Matt said.

Matt that morning told a story about Fran that Matt's brother, Michael, had told him. The story had become lore in Virginia swimming circles. Michael Miller was two years behind Fran at Virginia, and knew him well, and had witnessed the episode himself. In 2006, Virginia was vying for the Atlantic Coast Conference swimming championship. Virginia had won the meet three years in a row, but that year, on the last day of the three-day meet, Virginia was losing to Florida State. Every year, Virginia swimmers would paint a big V on their chests as a symbol of team unity and spirit. In 2006, on the last day, with Virginia losing, Coach Bernardino told all the swimmers to paint a smaller F and C on either side of the V. This was done to honor Fran Crippen, their team captain, and to motivate his teammates who loved him. Singling out an individual swimmer like this at Virginia had never been done before or since. But it worked that day. Virginia swimmers rallied unbelievably, with the FC on their chests, and won the meet, and the ACC championship.

Matt said Fran had tried out for the U.S. Olympic team in 2004, in the 400 meters, and narrowly missed. In 2008, he tried again to make the Olympic team, this time in a new event, the 10,000-meter open water swim. And after leading for the entire race, in a strong current at the Olympic trials, Fran paid the price and was caught at the end by swimmers who had been drafting him, and failed to make the team. But rather than complain, or give up, he redoubled his efforts, and established himself as the leading open water swimmer in America, and one of the best in the world. "I'm sure he's going to make the 2012 team," Matt said.

Matt innocently and admiringly told these stories about Fran on the car ride back to Philadelphia.

Thirteen days later, on October 23, 2010, near the end of an open-water swim in the Gulf of Oman, off the coast of Dubai in the United Arab Emirates, Fran Crippen drowned. The water temperature was simply too hot, over 86 degrees, and perhaps even closer to 90. The air temperature had been over 100. The conditions were simply unsafe to hold such a race. Fran Crippen, perhaps the fittest distance swimmer on the planet, was overcome by the heat, and lost consciousness, and drowned when no one noticed he'd gone under. The speculation was that he drowned within 500 yards of the finish of the six-mile race, though his body wasn't found until two hours later. Many other swimmers struggled that day with the heat, and several had to be hospitalized, and they complained bitterly that there were no safety boats around to help them when they began to struggle, no lifeguards watching the water. The death of Fran Crippen was an international tragedy and international story.

Fran, as his mother would say, could swim before he was potty-trained. He took to the water ever since he'd float in the bay in Avalon, New Jersey, off his grandparents' dock. He was the second of four children, the only boy, and all four Crippen children were fabulous swimmers. His older sister qualified for the 2000 Olympic team, and his younger sisters were both All-American collegiate swimmers. But Fran was the one who would light up a room, who was known in every circle he traveled simply as Fran, like a rock star, or movie star, never needing a last name. He was a natural athlete, good at everything. But swimming took Fran to the very top. When Fran was 15, he qualified for a junior national team that went to Barcelona. The coach was Mark Bernardino. Mark one morning after practice told his swimmers he was going to Gaudi's Cathedral Sagrada Familia, and Fran, being Fran, invited himself along, even though the young swimmers weren't supposed to leave the hotel. Fran told his coach he was sure Bernardino needed a translator or guide, and Bernardino immediately liked the boy. He was a tough, conniving, clever, street-wise kid from the Philly area, and Bernardino could relate. When Bernardino went back to mass on Sunday at that Gaudi cathedral, Fran said he had to go along, "to make sure you're granted forgiveness for contributing to the delinquency of minors!" How Fran's Italian Catholic mother back home loved hearing that Bernardino took her son to mass. When it came time to choosing a college, it was a no brainer that Fran would go to Virginia.

Fran was for so many reasons the best captain Mark Bernardino ever had in 37 years of coaching. He was the happiest kid. Everybody loved him. He could relate to anyone and everyone, on whatever level. He worked harder than anyone. After a monster practice, Bernardino would say "I kicked your ass," and Fran would say, "No way!" In fact, after doing a workout that nobody else could do, an insane workout, a workout that Bernardino would devise just for Fran, who could go harder, longer and faster than anyone, Fran would say to his coach, "I kicked your ass. You couldn't beat me!" And Fran would say it with a big smile. Fran was always smiling. He inspired his teammates not only with his work ethic and attitude, but because he always put team first. He sacrificed for team. He swam events that weren't his best because the team needed him to score points in those races. He would insist people on the team were as good as he was, were able to do what he could do, and urged them to stay with him. And he might take a slight bit off his own training, or speed, so that others in practice could stay with him, because he knew what a lift they would get thinking they had stayed with Fran. When he hugged Bernardino with that massive, perfect, Adonis-like body, with all the warmth and love that went along with his strength, the coach just felt safe. They became incredibly close. When Fran came to Bernardino's home, he didn't knock or ring a doorbell. The door would just fly open and Fran would bellow, "YO!!! Anybody home? What's up everybody!!" He loved Bernardino's young sons as his own brothers. He babysat them. He played so many hours of basketball with them in Bernardino's back yard that he wore out two backboards, and Bernardino put a small piece of one backboard into his casket at the funeral.

Fran's senior year in college he was team captain and Bernardino was straight-up with him. Coach didn't think the team had the talent to beat Florida State in that ACC championship meet. Bernardino told Fran he thought the team had grown complacent after winning several years in a row. But Fran was determined. He'd told the coach Virginia wasn't losing the team championship his final year, the year he was captain. "I don't think we have it," Bernardino told him. "No coach," he responded. "We're going to do it. I'm going to help them get there. We're not losing." And he would pour himself into practices and encourage his teammates. And on that last day of the meet, when Virginia was losing, Bernardino was wracking his brain, trying to think how he could motivate his team, and it came to him – the FC on either side of the V on the chests of his swimmers. In order to win, Bernardino needed perfection from his swimmers on the last day. He needed them to swim better than even they thought they could. Bernardino realized that swimming for themselves, or even for their university, might not be enough. "But by god they will want to win for Fran Crippen," Bernardino thought. "For him they'll give their last ounce of effort. And they did." Fran Crippen's mother, Pat, was at that meet in 2006 just as she was at virtually all his swim meets and saw the FC and remembers thinking, "Oh my God, he's going to be unfit to live with after this." Fran was anything but, of course. He was modest and thrilled for his team and gave others all the credit.

A few weeks before his death, he'd been voted Open Water Swimmer of the Year by USA swimming. And he was always the one pushing safety, looking out for the welfare of others. In August, just two months before his death, in an open water event in California, Fran actually turned around and swam the wrong way in the race to check on a friend, Alex Meyer, who was struggling with a stomach virus and had fallen back. Crippen found Meyer and let the ailing swimmer draft him the rest of the way. It was perhaps the cruelest irony that Fran Crippen's death would lead to making the sport safer for others. His tragedy illustrated the absence of safety standards for such events and the failure of international swimming officials to protect competitors. Those responsible for his safety and the safety of all swimmers failed him.

No one will ever know exactly what happened to Fran, and how he died. Clearly, adequate safety precautions and better judgment by race officials should have saved his life. But not lost on his own mother was the fact that what made Fran so great – his drive and determination and refusal to quit – also inevitably contributed to his death. In a long interview celebrating his life, Pat Crippen grew tearful and struggled as she said, "The thing that we love about Fran is the thing that I say if he had just….you know, if he had just…not…if he was just not so much that way, he'd still be with us. That's the hard thing. If he wasn't so driven…But that's who he was."

• • •

About 2,000 people came to Fran's funeral at St. Matthew Catholic Church in Conshohocken, Pennsylvania. Swimmers flew in from Europe and Hawaii. The crowd was so enormous that hundreds spilled over into the church school and watched on a video link.

Michael Miller flew home from Stanford for the funeral and the four Millers and Emily were in attendance. Many of the same swimmers that visited Matt in the hospital were there to show their love and support for

Fran Crippen. Matt, like his mother, was not a big crier, but he wept that morning. The day was horribly sad, and the death so obviously preventable. Matt was most upset seeing Mark Bernardino so devastated. Mark had been so instrumental in Matt's own survival, and Matt had come to love Mark Bernardino, there was no other way to describe it. And to see him suffering so now was deeply painful. Bernardino gave the eulogy, sharing anecdotes about Fran, and broke down several times in the process. All the Millers shared this love for Bernardino. Mike Miller had talked with Bernardino on the phone the evening before the funeral and shared something he knew only too well — "sometimes a good cry is the best we can do."

As Mike, Nancy, Michael and Emily sat in that church, not lost on any of them was how close they had come to feeling the grief the Crippen family was suffering now. Mike Miller, during the funeral mass, couldn't help but think how strange and unpredictable life could be. Matt had no right to live given what happened to him, and Fran Crippen had no reason to die. In Matt's case, everything that could have possibly gone right for him did, following the accident, and if anything had not, he would not have survived. In Fran's case, literally nothing went right, when it should have. That Mark Harris was in the last car was a miracle and a blessing and not something anyone could have expected. Matt Miller had no reason to expect help at the scene, his father thought, but Fran Crippen surely did.

Fran's longtime girlfriend and likely bride, Caitlin Regan, also spoke at the funeral, and Emily marveled at Caitlin's strength, that she could stand in front of so many, so soon, and speak so lovingly, with such composure. Caitlin shared with obvious pain that she and Fran were to meet in Rome after his race for a romantic vacation. Yet with humor and delight she also revealed a secret to their successful relationship: "He and I would settle any argument with a quick game of rock, paper, scissors." Emily could well imagine and relate to the pain Caitlin was feeling, but there was no way, Emily was sure, she could have shown such grace had this been Matt's funeral.

Michael was the member of the Miller family who knew Fran best. When Michael was a first-year walk-on, and Fran Crippen was the star of the Virginia swim team, Fran would treat him like an equal, give him rides, ask him how he was doing and take such an interest in Michael's life. And when Fran Crippen accepted Michael, the rest of the team followed suit. Michael had a deep faith in Christ, and he truly felt God had a role in saving his brother's life, and that God did answer prayers sometimes. He believed so many prayers said on behalf of his brother had influenced the outcome. But in church that day, Michael neither questioned God nor blamed Him for the death of Fran. No religion, Michael felt, had a perfect explanation for why God allowed horrible things to happen. Michael Miller did not see Fran's death as an act of God but as a failure by man. Michael believed God loves us enough to give us free will, that with free will we have the capacity to make bad choices, and that it took a bunch of people, primarily race organizers, making a lot of bad choices to allow Fran to die.

Matt didn't associate Fran's death with his own experience. He didn't ask God why his own life had been spared, but not Fran's. Matt just wasn't built that way. He just felt it was a terrible, terrible tragedy.

The death of Fran Crippen had another effect on all the Millers and those closest to Matt. It heightened their anxiety about Matt's Ironman in Cozumel. Emily's reaction was the strongest and most telling. When Matt phoned her on October 23rd, and told her the news of Fran's death, she told Matt he had to cancel his trip. He couldn't go. Emily had never met Fran Crippen herself, but the shock of his death was overwhelming. "Fran was sort of ever-present because people always talked about him," she said. And if something like this could happen to Fran, she reasoned, how could it be safe for Matt? Emily knew and everyone knew the water in Cozumel would be warm, maybe too warm. Matt quickly calmed Emily down, and assured her both that he was going, and that he was planning to be extremely careful. But in truth, Fran's death increased Matt's own anxiety about the event. He was in medical school now, at the University of Pennsylvania. What better symbol of his recovery than that? Was he being foolish? Was he pushing his luck? He decided on both counts that he was not, that this race was important to him. But he did recalibrate, and change his attitude. He was never going to Cozumel to win. But now, rather than just finish, his goal was going to be to finish strong. In other words, at no point would he be so exhausted that he would be in danger of collapse. He wanted to make sure that when he finished, he still had gas in his tank.

But this issue is what had everyone unnerved. In extreme endurance sports – whether it's a six-mile open water swim or an Ironman triathlon – there's such a fine line between fighting through pain and your body telling you something is horribly wrong. And it is a given in an Ironman triathlon that everyone will face pain. Matt had made a poor decision once before. He had gone back to Virginia Beach the previous spring, just before his college graduation, to run in the Shamrock Marathon. His parents had flown down to Virginia Beach to watch and support him. It had been a hot day, but not nearly as hot and humid as it would be in Cozumel. And Matt had failed to drink enough during the race. Even he knew something was seriously wrong in the last few miles but he kept running. When he crossed the finish line, he was ghostly white. His parents at the finish line urged him to go immediately to the medical tent, which he did, and where he remained for an hour and a half. He had an elevated heart rate that didn't drop for over 30 minutes. A cardiologist was in the tent that day taking care of Matt. When hearing about Matt's plans to go to medical school in the fall and do an Ironman at the same time, the cardiologist told Matt he simply couldn't do it. The doctor remembered his first year of medical school, and felt there just would be no way Matt could adequately prepare for the triathlon and succeed as a med student at the same time. Matt was not spooked by the doctor's comments that day, or by his own dehydration, and he got over the whole episode pretty quickly. His family and Emily did not.

"I know Matt's had minor problems in other races," Emily said days following Fran's death. "He gets too hot. He overexerts. I'm just not 100 percent confident that a person knows the difference between pushing himself to the max in exercising and knowing he needs to stop. Because when you're pushing yourself as hard as you possibly can you're obviously not going to feel good. You still may not know the difference between working your hardest and needing to stop." Matt talked with his parents and with Emily at length in November about how he was going to be sensible, take precautions, and keep safe. Nancy wasn't happy about the Ironman but she did not try to talk Matt out of Cozumel after Fran's death. She felt he knew what he was doing, understood the risks, and he would manage the event safely.

Mark Bernardino and Matt talked several times in the days and weeks after Fran's death, leading up to Cozumel, and Bernardino pounded the drum of caution more and harder than anyone. Bernardino had learned a lot about the fragility of life over the last two years, and he had a heightened awareness now about listening to the body. In fact, Bernardino had grown so conservative, so careful, that he tried to convince Matt that during the biking and running legs in Mexico he should repeatedly take his temperature, to make sure he wasn't overheating. Matt, the first-year medical student, explained to Bernardino that the only way to get a reliable reading was with a rectal thermometer, and that just wasn't going to happen. But Matt promised Bernardino, promised everyone, "I'm going to be very hypersensitive to my body in Cozumel. After what happened to Fran..."

And in the last month of preparation, he read endlessly about heat-acclimation, and tried his best to prepare himself for the heat and humidity. When he ran on the treadmill at 5:00 a.m. in the small gym in his apartment building, he turned up the thermostat full blast, and wore three layers of Under Armors, a hat and gloves. He put a humidifier right next to his indoor bike trainer, and as he pedaled he wore layers of clothing and his full-face helmet. His helmet, frankly, worried him. Cozumel was going to be hot, and wearing that helmet, the helmet he had promised everyone he would wear, was only going to make the ride that much hotter. Matt realized now that Cozumel was probably not the best choice for his Ironman. Cozumel was a lovely resort island off Mexico's Yucatan peninsula, a beautiful place to go on vacation or a honeymoon. But from a triathlete's point of view, the wind, heat, humidity, and high water temperature might be rather inhospitable. And coming from November in Philadelphia, the climate was going to be a shock. The best triathletes would arrive a week early, even two weeks, to give their bodies a chance to adjust. Because of medical school classes, Matt would be flying down on Thanksgiving, for a Sunday race. That was the best he could do.

Matt had chosen this race in part because he could minimize the time he would miss school. This, in fact, led to an amusing aside. The rules at Penn Med were pretty clear – all absences needed to be excused by the dean's office. Matt was only going to miss one day of classes, the Tuesday following Thanksgiving. There were no classes scheduled for that Monday. His plan was to spend Monday in Cozumel and recover after the race, and fly home Tuesday. And more than likely, with how well he was doing in school, nobody would have noticed or minded had he missed Tuesday classes. But Matt doesn't believe in evasion or deception. He was going to ask for permission, as the rules required, and he did. He filled out a form, asking for permission to be absent, giving as a reason that he'd be participating in an Ironman triathlon in Mexico. The dean's office, completely unaware of Matt's circumstances, saw this as an insufficient reason to miss class, and told him the absence would not be excused. Further, if Matt missed any more classes, he could lose points off his final grade. This frustrated Matt. He consulted his father, who encouraged him to provide a more detailed explanation to school officials. Matt wrote a lengthy e-mail to Stanley Goldfarb, the associate dean for clinical education, explaining what he'd been through and why this triathlon was important to him and all that he'd done in preparation. Matt explained that his professors were aware of his plans and supported him. Goldfarb, like most people in the medical school administration, had no idea about Matt's background. Moments after reading the e-mail, Goldfarb sent Matt a quick reply: "OK, Matt, you convinced me! A heck of a story with a happy ending. Stay safe and best of luck. You are excused."

Mike and Nancy, Michael and his now fiancée, Linda Liu, planned to make the trip to support Matt. Emily would not be going – not because she was opposed to him doing the triathlon, or afraid for him, but because the Thanksgiving holiday was her only chance to see her extended family, which was gathering in North Carolina. Because of all the tumult in her family, she really wanted to go and felt it was important. Matt understood and supported her. Emily wasn't the only one who wasn't going. Matt had also learned in recent weeks and months that he would be competing in Cozumel without any of the Three Musketeers, each of whom had dropped out, one by one. Tim Buckley had had knee surgery. Colin Kelton just had not been able to train adequately with the demands of work and family. Chris McIsaac's wife was expecting their third child any day, and he just couldn't risk being away. So D'Artagnan would do the Ironman alone.

―――――

CHAPTER TWELVE

M att Miller was one of about 2,300 competitors from many countries who came to Cozumel to compete in the Ironman. He was joining a tradition that began more than 30 years earlier and had grown and flourished around the world. In 2010, Cozumel was just one of 25 Ironman events worldwide, with nearly 50,000 competitors in total. And that was just the Ironman. Nearly two million men and women in the United States in 2010 participated in some triathlon somewhere, on roads or trails, in pools or oceans, lasting from less than an hour to nearly a day, according to the Sporting Goods Manufacturers Association.

How the sport began is remarkable for its innocence and lack of any grand vision. The first modern triathlon, in San Diego in 1974, was conceived as something fun, a family event. And the first official Ironman events in Hawaii in 1978, started as a mom-and-pop event. Both events illustrate so well that the greatest achievements start with a simple idea, or a gut feeling, and with someone who has the gumption to bring that idea to life.

In the early 1970s, the San Diego Track Club, a group of men and women who liked to run, held an annual event known as the Dave Pain Birthday Biathlon. Dave Pain was the founder of masters running, and this was just a fun event held on Mission Bay in which a 4.5-mile run was followed by a 300-yard swim. Jack Johnstone, a track club member, had been a high school and college swimmer, and had only recently taken up jogging in the early 1970s along with millions of Americans. He wanted to lengthen the swim portion of the Dave Pain Birthday Biathlon. He actually envisioned several legs, alternating runs and swims, and some of the running could be done on the beach in bare feet. The event's organizer suggested Johnstone call another club member, Don Shanahan, who also had some ideas for changing the event. So Johnstone called Shanahan and learned that Shanahan wanted to add a bicycle leg. "I wasn't too thrilled with the suggestion," Johnstone wrote years ago, "having never cycled competitively (I didn't even own a bike). But what the hell, I thought, let's go for it. We decided to call the event the Mission Bay Triathlon."

They published a brief notice in the San Diego Track Club newsletter, September 1974:

RUN, CYCLE, SWIM: TRIATHLON SET FOR 25TH

The First Annual? Mission Bay Triathlon, a race consisting of segments of running, bicycle riding, and swimming, will start at the causeway to Fiesta Island at 5:45 P.M. September 25. The event will consist of 6 miles of running (longest continuous stretch, 2.8 miles), 5 miles of bicycle riding (all at once), and 500 yards of swimming (longest continuous stretch, 250 yards). Approximately 2 miles of running will be barefoot on grass and sand. Each participant must bring his own bicycle. Awards will be presented to the first five finishers. For further details contact Don Shanahan (488-4571) or Jack Johnstone (461-4514).

The trophy maker called Johnstone and asked him how to spell triathlon; he couldn't find it in any dictionaries. Johnstone figured since he was inventing the word, he got to decide. "Given the spellings PENTATHLON, HEPTATHLON, and DECATHLON," Johnstone wrote in an interview on www.triathlonhistory.com, "I guess there wasn't really much choice, but it seemed like a lot of power at the time."

John and Judy Collins did not consider themselves athletes at all. John Collins was a U.S. Naval Academy graduate and officer stationed in San Diego, and their two children swam on a local swim team. John and Judy decided to try lap swimming themselves in early 1973, and enjoyed it, but were slow and anything but competitive. Another lap swimmer and swim team parent showed John and Judy a flier on the very afternoon of the triathlon, and said she was going over. The Collins family – John, Judy, Kristin and Michael, ages 38, 35, 13 and 12 – decided to join her.

"We started out running 2.8 miles," recalled Judy. "When we finished that, our bikes were leaning against the car. We biked two loops that added up to five miles, then leaned the bikes back against the car and ran across the causeway, and threw our shoes in a black bag, and swam across the inlet, to a finish lit by headlights and a fire on the beach." Judy said their daughter swam butterfly stroke most of the way, to the amazement of most participants, who were runners, and were struggling to keep their heads above water.

Within a year, John Collins was transferred to Hawaii and the Collins family relocated there. They joined the Waikiki Swim Club and John and Judy also joined the Mid-Pacific Road Runners Club. The Collins adults still didn't consider themselves competitive athletes, but they loved exercising, and what they lacked in speed they compensated for in endurance, enjoying longer and longer events. Judy realized through her own experience that the human body was built for endurance, and was capable of incredible things, but most people simply weren't aware of that. Both John and Judy completed the 2.4 mile Waikiki Roughwater Swim and the 26.2 mile Honolulu Marathon. On Mother's Day in 1977, Judy swam 9 miles from Lanai to Maui, from one Hawaiian Island to another.

At the time, the Mid-Pacific Road Runners and the Waikiki Swim Club held an annual run-swim biathlon competition at Ala Moana Beach Park on Oahu. It was considered a sprint event – a three mile run and 700 yard swim, roughly. If the runners won big one year, the swim was lengthened the next. If the swimmers won big one year, the swim was shortened the next. In 1977, John and Judy were co-chairs of the event, and they began dreaming up the idea of changing and expanding it into a triathlon, and not a short triathlon, but an endurance event.

John Collins had the brainstorm. Why not take existing events and do all on the same day? Do the 2.4 mile Waikiki Roughwater Swim, then the Honolulu Marathon, and conclude it with the Bike Around Oahu, a 112-mile loop around Hawaii's big island. John and Judy decided on the order of events – swim, bike, run – for the most practical reason: they wanted swimmers out of the water and bikes off the road before dark. John figured the event wouldn't seem too crazy to people if it combined events they already were familiar with. Still, said Judy, "there was an outrageousness to it, and a little bit of curiosity if we could pull it off."

Then there was the matter of what to call it. This again was John's idea. He was an engineer at the naval shipyard. There was a civilian of Japanese descent who worked at the shipyard and ran every day. Whether he ran one mile or 30, he always ran the same speed, an 8:15 mile pace. And he could run all day. Around the shipyard, among his coworkers, he was simply called Ironman. John decided that whoever finished this triathlon, this incredible endurance feat, would be called Ironman. He even designed the Ironman trophy.

John and Judy and another couple, good friends of like mind, organized the event for February 18, 1978 and charged $5 per person to cover costs. Fifteen people competed in that first Ironman, including John Collins. Early on in the biking leg, he asked himself, "Whose idea was this?" After biking halfway around the island, he decided to eat some chili, which he quickly discovered was a very bad idea, throwing up. On the run, his legs were dead. He'd read about a marathoner who would stash beer on the course, and John Collins thought a beer might help him, so he stopped and bought one. Another very bad idea. Still, he finished: 17 hours and 38 seconds. His wife was waiting for him, in the dark, in their VW van.

The next year, in 1979, more than 40 people planned on doing the second annual Ironman, but bad weather forced a one-day delay, and all but 15 had to cancel. Still, Sports Illustrated covered the event, and after its story appeared John Collins received shoeboxes full of letters from people all over the world who wanted to compete. ABC's Wide World of Sports asked John and Judy if it could cover the event in 1980, and the event became a worldwide sensation when a woman who had led for the entire day collapsed, and crawled the last 100 yards across the finish line. This dramatic finish helped make the Ironman Triathlon a worldwide sensation. Just as the event exploded in popularity, the Collins family left Hawaii and ceded control of the event to others. John and Judy are now retired, in their 70s, living most of the year in Panama, where the climate reminds them so much of Hawaii.

They still do smaller triathlons and other endurance events, and are very proud of what they've helped to create. In their own small way, they had a role in Matt Miller's recovery. They started an event that helped motivate him to heal, that would become a symbol of his own personal triumph. And no doubt there were countless others like Matt.

• • •

The night before the Ironman, Matt couldn't sleep. So many things were keeping him awake. Some were universal among competitors everywhere: Was he ready? Could he do it? Would his body hold up over a combined 140 miles of swimming, biking and running? And some of his anxieties were unique, such as a concern about his helmet. All contestants were required to leave their helmets and cycling shoes on hooks overnight, near the first transition tent. Matt's full-face helmet looked so unlike a traditional bike helmet that he feared race officials might for some reason confiscate it. What if they took it? Matt could only ride if he had a full-face helmet. As he tossed and turned in his hotel room, which he was sharing with his brother, Matt decided he needed a little inspiration. To calm himself and provide some perspective, he started reading the e-mails he'd received from friends and strangers in the last two years. People wrote that he had inspired them, but at this critical moment they were inspiring him right back. One of the e-mails included a quote from Winston Churchill, which Matt felt was perfect for an Ironman: "Success is not final; failure is not fatal. It is the courage to continue that counts."

Matt wasn't sure how much sleep he actually got that night, but he was up at 3:45 a.m. to throw some jelly on four English muffins and inhale them in his room. Moments later he roused his brother out of bed. Matt needed Michael's help. Michael got a Sharpie marker and drew a big V on Matt's chest, and a smaller F and C just below the point of the V. This was something Matt had been thinking about almost since the moment he heard about Fran's death, as a way to honor him. Matt had asked his brother whether he thought it was a good idea, whether it somehow might be disrespectful to Virginia swimming, since Matt had only been on the team for a year, or to the Crippens. Michael didn't think so and suggested Matt ask Mark Bernardino. A couple of weeks before he left for Mexico, Matt called Mark one afternoon. Bernardino was on the pool deck, running a practice. Bernardino generally wouldn't answer the phone during practices, but he could see it was Matt, and they had been talking about his preparations for the Ironman. "I'm going to ask you a really hard question," Matt began, "and you don't have to say yes." Matt told him he'd like to wear the V and FC on his chest during the Ironman. Bernardino responded instantly. "I think that's one of the greatest honors you can pay Fran," he said. "And Fran will watch over you and wearing that FC on your chest and having him watch over you, you will be completely safe. You don't have anything to worry about. You'll be fine. Please wear that FC. That means everything to me. And if Fran were here it would mean everything to him."

That settled that. Matt told Emily, and his brother, but no one else, not even his parents. He wasn't doing this for attention, just out of respect.

After Michael drew the letters on that morning, Matt pulled up his one-piece triathlon body suit, sliding the straps over his shoulders and covering up the letters. Matt then went down to the lobby of his hotel to get on the 5:00 a.m. bus to the starting area. Michael went back to sleep.

In the pitch black, on a hot, stuffy bus choked with competitors, Matt rode silently to the start. His dad went with him, sitting beside him, carrying Matt's bicycle pump. The symbolism was pretty powerful. His parents had been beside him, supporting him, from the very start of this journey, really all his life. Matt had pumped up his tires the day before, but he wanted to check them again that morning. Matt got off the bus and walked into the transition area. His father wasn't allowed in, only contestants, so Matt took the pump and agreed to meet his father at a designated spot at 6:15. The starter's horn was set to blast at 7:00 a.m. The race was to begin at a public park on the beach, and the parking area was filled with 2,300 bicycles. The first thing Matt did was check on his helmet and cycling gear – exactly where he had left them. That was a big relief. The bags and bicycles were labeled with each contestant's number, and arranged in numerical order, so competitors could find their bags and bikes. Matt's number was 274, and he found his bike easily. Even though he'd covered the seat with plastic, it was soaked from the humidity overnight. "This temperature is perfect," Matt said. "Maybe the sun won't come up today." In the pre-dawn darkness, Matt fiddled with his bike, checking tires and gears and stuffing energy bars and assorted nutritional pastes and snacks in every pouch and cranny. He had equipped his bike with two 24-ounce water bottles and with a streamlined 40-ounce water tank, with a long tube that would serve as a straw. He figured he would refill as necessary – his goal was to drink 32 ounces an hour on the bike. Other riders were all around him, fussing with their own bikes, and one after the other gratefully borrowed his bicycle pump. Norah Jones was playing on the public address, filling the pre-dawn with her sweet voice. Norah Jones was not triathlon music, Matt noted. But then, more appropriately, *Sunday Bloody Sunday* by U2 filled the air. Matt was concentrating too hard on getting ready to think about song lyrics or their symbolism. But he had already survived one bloody Sunday. Was this going to be another? He would soon find out.

Around 6:00 a.m., confident his bike was ready, he went for a 10-minute run, just to get loose, and to lose a few of his jitters. By 6:25 a.m. Matt met his mother, father, Michael and Linda in the designated spot. In the last hour, darkness had turned to light and what had been a peaceful parking area was now teeming with competitors and well-wishers.

"OK gorgeous," said his mother, giving him a hug and kiss.

His father kissed Matt on the top of his crew cut. Matt had buzzed his head as part of his acclimation effort. Then Mike Miller made a gesture in sign language, "I love you." Matt had started doing this in the hospital when his jaw had been wired shut. Two years later, he and his father had never stopped.

Michael zipped up Matt's triathlon suit in the back, the finishing touch, like a husband zipping his wife's dress before a night out. There were lots of brothers in Cozumel doing the triathlon together, and fathers and sons, and husbands and wives, and Matt had jokingly asked Michael a year ago to train and join him, and Michael's response, knowing an Ironman was just far too extreme for him, had been a level-headed, "Never, ever."

Matt disappeared into the crowd and his father said, "Now if we can only have a happy ending."

• • •

Before 7:00 a.m., 2,300 heads in orange bathing caps were bobbing in the turquoise sea, a beautiful sight, waiting for the starting horn. Matt was lost among them. His strategy was to get near the front – swimming was his strongest leg – and get ahead of the crowds and mayhem, settle into a smooth stroke, and relax. He knew and everyone knew the start of the swim was dangerous. A swimmer died in the Schuylkill River in Philadelphia the previous summer during the short Philadelphia Sprint Triathlon. The victim had been a middle-aged man, a decent swimmer. Perhaps he'd been kicked or trampled by other swimmers. Nobody would ever know what happened. But Matt knew now his best bet was to get out quick.

The island of Cozumel is situated at the western end of the Caribbean Sea. Tourism officials like to say Cozumel has a Mexican heart and Caribbean soul. The east side of the island faces the open Caribbean, with substantial waves, and the strongest winds. All the resort hotels are on the western side of the island, along with spectacular reefs, and a much calmer sea. This body of water is officially known as the Cozumel Channel, and is about seven miles wide. Across the channel is the mainland, the Yucatan Peninsula and the better known resort city of Cancun. The swimming portion of the Ironman would be on this west side of the island, in the channel, paralleling the beach. Once the horn fired, swimmers treading water would swim north along the shoreline for just over half a mile. They would round a buoy, head 100 yards out to sea, round another buoy, and then swim a mile south, again paralleling the beach. They would round a third giant red buoy, swim back 100 yards toward the shore, round a final buoy and then swim the last half mile heading for home. In essence, they would swim a long narrow rectangle.

Mike, Nancy, Michael and Linda found a place on the beach, maybe 100 yards from where the swim would start and finish. That was about as close as they could get. It was impossible to distinguish one swimmer from another

– one orange cap looked like every other. But they hoped to spot Matt as he finished. When he emerged from the water, he would be wearing those big triathlon goggles. Most swimmers would be wearing the more typical Speedo-style racing goggles.

The horn blasted.

Matt was able to get out quick, and found a pack of swimmers that he felt was cruising at a comfortable pace, and fell in. For most competitors, swimming is the quickest of the three legs of an Ironman. But more important than how fast you swim is how much energy you conserve. Competitors want to be efficient in their stroke, and Matt was doing his best just to relax and remain smooth. The water was 83 degrees, and actually felt perfect rather than too hot. Matt wasn't paying much attention to the beautiful fish all around him, just concentrating on his stroke, his rhythm. He felt a few stings from jellyfish, but these were mild and of minimal significance. At one point during the swim it did cross his mind how relieved he was to know that Dr. Singer had cemented into place his permanent and final set of teeth just a few weeks earlier and there was no chance that his teeth could be lost at sea. Overall Matt was feeling good, comfortable, and well aware of how much nicer it was to swim in this calm, clear sea than to do endless flipturns in an indoor pool.

Even though his family had been so nervous about the swim for weeks, when the morning finally arrived, standing on the beach, they were all calmer than they expected to be. The water was beautiful, not as warm as they had feared. The start appeared to go smoothly, the crush of orange caps moving up the beach, gradually thinning out. The family had come to feel that if Matt could just start out safely, the swim would probably be the leg they'd worry about the least on such a hot and humid day. His family knew if all went well he'd probably be near the front of the pack of swimmers, so they were watching carefully as each swimmer emerged from the sea. And there he was. Matt looked strong. The four of them cheered and screamed his name but of course he couldn't hear them and they were too far away for him to see them. Mike and Michael both counted Matt among maybe the first 50 or 60 swimmers, certainly among the first 100, which was fabulous.

Matt felt confident as he climbed the ladder onto the dock, peeled off his cap and goggles, and dashed past the cheering crowds toward his bicycle and the transition area. He figured he was near the front and he felt great. So far, so good.

The family scurried from the beach to the road a couple hundred yards away. They wanted to be standing right along the railing as Matt emerged from the transition area, and began his bike ride.

Matt grabbed his biking gear and helmet and walked into the first transition tent. He sat in a chair, and drank a recovery drink, and toweled off and lathered himself up carefully with suntan lotion. He was a fair-skinned young man coming straight from a Philadelphia November into the Caribbean sun, so no amount of lotion was too much. He put on his cycling shoes and gloves and mixed two bottles of sports drink for the long ride, to go along with the water tank on his bike. He put on his helmet, which made him look more like a hockey goalie than a bike racer, and jogged out of the tent to find his bike and start his next leg.

Leaning against the railing along the road, waiting for Matt to appear, Mike Miller got an e-mail on his BlackBerry. It wasn't even 8:00 a.m.

"A 52:36 swim! What a start! Looks as if he was first in his age group out of the water. And 44th overall. Incredible!"

The e-mail was from Chris McIsaac, who was following the race online at his home outside Philadelphia. Matt, along with every contestant, was wearing a computer chip. And what would become clear very quickly was that people thousands of miles away, in their slippers and sipping coffee in their living rooms, would be able to know how well Matt Miller was doing – his place, his times, his splits – far better than his family which was there in Cozumel, battling the crowds of spectators.

Emily was also watching from North Carolina, and posted on Facebook: "Emily Privette is SO excited for Matt Miller who is doing his FIRST IRONMAN RIGHT NOW!!" And right around that time, a little more old-fashioned and simply using a telephone, Merrily Stilwell, the Vanguard receptionist with MS, called her beloved Pink Sisters and asked them, once again, to please pray for Matt.

Riders were streaming out of the transition area, onto the road, like bees flying out of a hive. But Matt was easy to spot with his zebra-striped full-face helmet. The Millers and Linda cheered wildly and loudly for him as he pedaled past. He couldn't really turn his head and look at them – the road was dense with cyclists – but he heard them and gave them a big thumbs-up as he pedaled off into the headwind and rapidly climbing temperature.

The bike portion of this Ironman was three laps around the island – mostly out in the open, along the water. So Matt and other riders would face headwinds, crosswinds and tailwinds. Matt expected the bike leg to last from five to seven hours, or longer. As he disappeared into the distance, the family went back to their hotel for breakfast. It was going to be a long day for them, too, and they figured they'd catch up with him on the bike in two or three hours. As they were just sitting down, Mike got another e-mail, this one from Tim Buckley: *"Unbelievable swim (Mike, I told you he would kill it). If you didn't know he had to put on that elaborate head gear, you would think he took a nap at T1 (10 minutes!). I hope he remembered the sunscreen."* "T1" was triathlon-speak for first transition area, and most competitors hustled through it in two, three or four minutes. But Matt, by comparison, had taken his time. Mike Miller got another e-mail a moment later from Bill McNabb, who'd been copied on the earlier e-mails: "Amazing. We'll be watching all day." McNabb sent another: "The swim was faster than many pros and only 6 minutes behind Andy Potts. Incredible!" Andy Potts was a former collegiate swimmer at Michigan and a professional triathlete, a favorite to win the Cozumel Ironman. Finishing only six minutes behind Potts over 2.4 miles was impressive. A moment later, another e-mail, from McIsaac again: "I'd need a jetski to get that close to Potts. Amazing swim."

Matt anticipated well before the race began that the bike leg for him would be the hardest. With the wind and the heat and the distance, not to mention the helmet, he believed if he could just get through the bike leg without cramping, without dehydrating, without completely wearing himself out, he'd get through the marathon safely as well. The bike leg had worried him the most. And the Friday before the race, as he was preparing himself and his gear in Cozumel, he received some excellent advice from Ken Glah.

Glah, 46, was from West Chester, Pennsylvania, also in the Philadelphia area, and was a former professional triathlete. Glah had finished in 26 straight Ironman triathlons in Hawaii, and in more than 60 overall. He had won six, three in Brazil, two in New Zealand, and one in Canada. In 2002, he started Endurance Sports Travel, making arrangements for competitors and families at triathlons and other endurance events around the world. After more than 20 years, he knew from experience what was involved in traveling abroad with triathlon gear and families in tow. He and his small company were handling arrangements for 90 people in Cozumel, including the Miller family. Since they had no idea what to expect in Cozumel, the Millers had signed up and let Glah handle their arrangements. Glah shared his strategy with Matt on that Friday before the race, and told Matt his goal should be to ride each of the three loops around the island faster than the one before. Glah told Matt that pumped-up cyclists would be passing him left and right on the first lap, and that was okay. Matt needed to fight the urge to be competitive with them, especially if he was feeling good. Glah reminded Matt an Ironman is an endurance event, to hydrate and pace himself. So Matt kept that in mind as he pedaled off on the first loop, as other riders were indeed passing him left and right, and almost everyone who went by stared at Matt's helmet.

As Matt circled the island the first time, he just tried to stay alert, stay calm and hold back the throttle, remembering what Ken Glah had told him. In the first few miles, when he hit some rough pavement, one of his water bottles fell off, lost for good. Race organizers wisely had arranged water stops every ten miles on the bike leg, and Matt slowed at many of those to refill his tank and remaining bottle. He tried to suck down about 30 to 35 ounces of fluid an hour according to plan. And probably every 20 to 30 miles he grabbed a cold water bottle as he rolled through a water station and squirted it through the vent holes in his helmet – another recommendation from Ken Glah, and one Matt truly appreciated every time he did it.

Knowing their day was going to be nearly as long as Matt's, the family wasn't in a huge hurry to get back to the bike course. They could have just walked up the road from their resort hotel and watched, but they wanted to go back to the center of town and spend the day there. That way they could watch both the cycling and running portions, which overlapped only in the town center. That area was also where the finish was located.

The Millers were on the bike course by 11:15, and hoped to see Matt ride by as he was just beginning his third loop, at about the 75 mile mark. When 11:30 came and went, the family felt maybe they had missed him. It was hot standing along the road. The temperature by then had climbed to 90, with high humidity. They were anxious. Had something gone wrong? They thought Matt must be okay because they'd received an e-mail from McIsaac which read: "First bike split is in – Matt averaged 19 mph over the first 32.5 miles." That was great news. But at that rate Matt should have been passing by them at any moment. They kept craning their necks, looking to see cyclists as they came into view, looking for the rider with the full-face helmet. They kept glancing at their watches. They tried to keep the darkest thoughts out of their minds, and stay positive. But waiting and wondering was no fun, especially in a blazing sun.

But then there he came, at 11:45, looking strong. They screamed, but Matt didn't acknowledge them.

"I don't think he saw us," said his mother.

"But he definitely heard us," said his father.

Matt saw them, but he couldn't wave or acknowledge them in any way because they'd foolishly parked themselves on a turn, one of only four on the entire course. Matt needed both hands on his handle bars, to turn safely and avoid wiping out.

"He's moving pretty well," said his mother.

The others agreed and were comforted.

Shortly after noon, they got another e-mail from McIsaac: "21.4 mph over the next 39 miles."

"Strong!" e-mailed Colin Kelton, a moment later.

Both Kelton and McIsaac had figured how to track Matt not only on their computers, but on their BlackBerrys, and were following the race literally all day. In fact, sitting in church on Sunday morning with his family, Kelton kept thinking about Matt, and where he should be. Kelton kept wanting to check his BlackBerry, between hymns, or during the sermon, but these men are nothing if not disciplined and he restrained himself. But as soon as services ended, Kelton saw Matt was out of the water, and onto the bike.

McIsaac checked the results as he made pancakes in the morning for his kids. He checked when he returned from his own bike ride. That afternoon, his wife wanted to go out one last time before the baby, expected any day. So they went to see the latest Harry Potter movie. McIsaac kept looking at race updates during the movie, annoying his wife, who "disciplined me twice for checking my BlackBerry," McIsaac said. He finally got smart and said he had to go to the bathroom, and went out to the lobby to check the results and send an e-mail update to Mexico.

The Three Musketeers all felt badly that they had bailed on Matt. Seeing how well he was doing, they were just thrilled for him.

Matt's preparations and strategy were paying off. On his third and final bike lap around the island, the rider in the full-face helmet was doing most of the passing, startling one rider who later blogged, "I said out loud, 'WTF?'"

People were lined along the bike route all the way around the island. Crowds were thickest through the island's little downtown, where the Millers had chosen to watch. One service Ken Glah provided his clients was transportation to and from the race, and he also set up tents along the course where families and supporters could watch. One tent was across from where the bike leg ended, and the Millers went there hoping to see Matt dismount. Maybe they could cheer him and see him head into the second transition area before beginning his run. Because so many streets were roped off, and because of the crowds, and because they didn't know exactly where they were going, the Millers ran into a few dead ends and took more than half an hour to find the tent. They expected Matt around 1:15, or maybe 1:30. But, again, as the clock kept ticking and Matt was nowhere in sight, their anxiety grew. The professionals like Andy Potts were the first ones to finish the bike leg, and some of them were so efficient, so into saving time, that they had slipped their feet right out of their bike shoes, which remained clipped into the pedals. They would just stop, hop off, and run toward the next transition tent. Many of the first riders looked good, but some looked absolutely spent. And these were among the leaders. Several dismounted and just collapsed. They just called it a day, and didn't even entertain the idea of running. The Millers were anxious as they watched, hot and tired. This was a very tense moment, and it showed on their faces, but they were still far from panic or alarm. There was no cause for that. Around 1: 45 p.m., the rider in the full-face helmet finally appeared. Or at least it felt like finally. Yet he seemed to be rolling confidently and comfortably along, and dismounted without a problem. Mike and Nancy, Michael and Linda waved and cheered Matt as he passed by their tent, and he gave them a celebratory wave, as if to say, "112 miles in the Mexican heat? No big deal." Matt was still thinking like a competitor and jogged to the transition tent, picking up on the way a second bag, this one filled with his running shoes and sun visor. Matt already now had some serious sunburn on his shoulders, arms and legs, but he didn't seem to notice or care. He disappeared into the second transition tent, found a seat, and again took his time. He lathered himself up with lotions and creams, took several long, cold drinks, pulled off his bike shoes and put on his running shoes. Others came and went. Matt snacked on some energy bars, which he'd also been eating throughout the bike ride to keep up his calories. He finally emerged from the tent to begin the marathon, looking relatively fresh and composed. "I'll see you in a few hours," he said, as he trotted off. It was around 2:00 p.m.

The e-mails started coming in.

From McIsaac: "He did it! Third segment completed at 20.47 mph. He's in T2 now."

From McNabb, three minutes later: "Amazing results. Looks like he has put together a very consistent and controlled race. Bravo!"

From McIsaac again, 11 minutes later: "Final bike split: 5:37:44. 19.9 avg pace. Beat my Coeur d'Alene time by 21 mins!"

The Millers decided to head into a restaurant designated by Endurance Sports Travel and get a drink, a quick bite to eat, and some shade. In what seemed like no time another e-mail from McIsaac came: Matt had run the first four miles of the marathon in 7:37 pace. The Millers were thrilled and nervous at the same time.

"I hope he's not going too fast," said his mother. "He's got 26 miles to go. Shouldn't he slow down?"

"He may have gone easy on the bike, saving it for the run," said his dad.

The marathon course was simple and straightforward. Competitors ran along a main boulevard from the downtown out to the airport. That was almost 4.4 miles. They turned around and ran back, an 8.8 mile lap. The runners would simply do three laps, out and back. The result would be a full marathon, 26.2 miles. The boulevard was lined with palm trees. On one side was the port, where cruise ships docked. On the other side of the boulevard were the little trinket shops catering to the tourists coming off those cruise ships. Michael and Linda walked about a mile down the boulevard, and found a bench on which to sit and wait for Matt. Mike and Nancy stayed closer to the finish.

A few things had become very clear watching this Ironman. Matt was among the very youngest competitors. He was 22, and most were in their late 20s or 30s, all the way up into their 70s. Nearly one-third of the competitors were women. And men and women competing in that triathlon came in every conceivable shape and size. By the time most of these runners reached the marathon stage, they were struggling, their strides stiff and labored, facial expressions frozen in pain.

Matt appeared to be moving relatively smoothly, though pain was evident on his face. As he completed the first lap, eight miles, asked how he was feeling, he shrugged. That was the best he could do.

As Matt headed out on his second lap, at around the 10-mile mark, he passed Michael and Linda, and told them, "don't die." Clearly Matt was locked in his own little world and talking to himself. Michael thought his brother looked pretty good, and had been feeling confident about Matt all day. Michael knew his brother had trained well, and planned a sensible approach to the day, as much as sensible and triathlon could ever be associated with one another. Michael and Linda just sat on that bench, enjoying a lazy afternoon, watching the world go by and waiting for Matt to come by them again in another hour or so as he finished his second lap. Sure enough, there he was, nearing 17 miles. Michael and Linda cheered him, praised him and encouraged him. The best Matt could muster was a nod.

"Definitely more tired than the first pass," said Michael. It was 4:10 p.m. He'd been going since 7:00 a.m.

For Matt, finishing up that second lap, turning around and trudging out again to start the third – this was the worst and lowest time of the day for him. His legs were leaden, and he was sunburned, chafing and blistered, and his stomach was misbehaving badly. But as miserable as he felt, he knew this was a healthy misery. He had felt worse before, much worse – as in the last six miles of that marathon in Virginia Beach. That was a scary misery, and he knew his mind wasn't working right. Now, though in pain, he was still well-oriented, well aware of where he was, what he was doing, how he was feeling. Overall he knew this was good, that he was in control and not in any danger. But he was hurting.

Several times during his long day of endurance, but particularly in this most challenging stretch, Matt thought about the V and FC on his chest and about Fran Crippen. These thoughts motivated him, gave purpose and meaning to this pain, kept him going. Maybe Fran really was watching over him, as Bernardino said, because Matt felt safe and he felt strong, and never for a moment thought about quitting.

Matt had done all he could to prepare for the race. And he'd been eating all day long, energy bars and fruit and protein pastes, to keep up his energy level. He had also resolved, before the triathlon started, to walk for 30 to 90 seconds at every water stop in the marathon, and to drink at every stop. And he was keeping to his plan. The water stops were set up every kilometer, and Matt just pushed himself from one water stop to another, one kilometer to the next, knowing he'd get a short break, something to drink. This was not only prudent but great motivation. At each water stop, he'd throw ice down into his body suit and up on his head. And only one kilometer until he'd get to do it again!

• • •

As Matt rounded the last turn, just 4 miles to the finish, the sun was beginning to set – the day had come and gone. As the shadows lengthened, so did Matt's perspective. Matt began to feel stronger, more confident with each step now. For the whole race, Matt had focused on the moment, on his body, on taking care of himself. But he was growing more certain that he would finish, and finish strong. And he started thinking now in these last few miles about his longer journey – how far he'd come, what he was about to accomplish, and the doctors, friends and family who had healed him, cheered him, and helped him get here. With a mile to go, he passed his brother and Linda, and they were screaming and jumping and cheering, and that fueled him like a booster rocket. Matt picked up the pace, his fastest mile of the day, and he didn't even realize it. He grew more emotional. In that last mile, more than 50 faces, maybe 100, flashed through his mind like a slide show. There was Emily of course, who was really there with him even though she wasn't. He thought of the doctors at UVA who had saved him, the rescue workers on the mountain, some of whom he'd met since the accident. He thought of Bernardino leading him up the stairwells, and of many of the swimmers who visited him. He thought about his grandparents and his uncles and aunts and his classmates at UVA and at Penn Med. He saw Mark and Mary Ann Harris on their front walk, and Dr. Hanks in his clinic. Faces just kept flashing before him, Rudy and Chris, the Vanguard crew, even Merrily Stilwell and her butterflies. He felt gratitude, and excitement, for in a way all these people were right there with him, and he wouldn't be closing in on the finish line were it not for each and every one of them. Two years ago almost to the day he'd left the hospital. And now he was about to finish an Ironman triathlon, and probably a lot faster than he or anyone else ever imagined he could go. He was just feeling so….happy, so free. Maybe it was delirium, as much from exhaustion as from relief. He knew now he was going to accomplish his goal. He felt it was in reach. He felt strong and in control. The streets were lined with people, screaming and cheering in support. He was searching the crowd for his parents. He really wanted to see them. This had been their journey, too, that was coming to an end. This was their triumph as well as his.

Mike and Nancy had found a spot right on the rail, about 40 yards from the finish line. The long day of worry and anxiety had worn them down, too. They knew the last eight miles of the marathon would be the hardest. They kept leaning over the railing now, craning their necks, looking down the road, trying to see him approach. Where was he? Was he OK? Michael called them, and said he'd seen Matt with a mile to go, and Matt looked strong.

Mike, so excited now, found himself thinking about the day they left the hospital, what he considered maybe the greatest day of his life, seeing Matt walk out, raising that fist in triumph. Mike had that same sense of euphoria now as he searched the dusk for his son.

"THERE HE IS!" screamed Nancy.

"Matt, Matt!" They both yelled. He turned and acknowledged them, a quick smile and thumbs up as he passed. Matt was so glad he had seen them, so happy to know they were there, at the finish, to share the moment with him. He turned and looked ahead now, and saw himself on the giant screen above the finish, much larger than life. There were grandstands on each side of the finish, filled with cheering fans. In his last few strides, Matt heard the announcer, proclaim to the world, "Matthew Miller of the United States, you...are...an...IRONMAN!"

Matt crossed the line and stopped. He stood tall, arms stretched out to the heavens, face skyward, and surrendered himself to the moment. He was happy, proud, grateful – and so glad it was over. He just stood there, still, for the longest moment, eyes closed.

"We did it," he told himself. "We did it."

His time was 10 hours, 30 minutes, 12 seconds – 209th overall.

His marathon was 3:42:26.

He was sitting in a chair in the recovery area, eating a slice of pizza, still wearing his sunglasses in the dark, when his parents reached him. The recovery area was restricted to competitors only. But Matt was against a fence, so he was able to stand and throw his arms around his parents in a three-way hug.

"Matthew Miller, you're unbelievable," his mother said. The thin line of stress that had been her mouth all day had blossomed into the broadest smile. The light from Nancy Miller's face was enough to illuminate the dark.

His father kissed his forehead. "How do you feel?" Mike Miller asked.

Matt was a well-mannered and respectful young man, who seldom swore, but this occasion called for it, and in a euphoric, triumphant and celebratory way, with the widest grin, Matt replied, "I'm f– -ing *tired*!"

Nancy reached out and rubbed the fuzz of his crew cut. People all around Matt were sprawled on the ground, or collapsed in ice baths, or hugging and screaming in celebration. Matt wasn't even breathing hard, and seemed to have stopped sweating already, within minutes of the finish. He had pulled down the top half of his triathlon suit, to relieve the chafing and sunburn. One could not see any signs of the V and FC. They appeared to have been worn away by water, sweat, and 140 miles of friction. But those letters, and the spirit they represented, had done their job. Matt asked for his father's cell phone and first called Emily. She had been glued to her computer, refreshing the screen constantly, to get the latest results, but there must have been a delay of a few moments, because she was surprised to get Matt's call. She didn't know he had finished, though as she talked to him his results popped up on her screen. She told him she loved him and was proud of him and happy for him and wished she could be there with him, but he couldn't really hear much of anything because the recovery area was pulsing with a salsa band and with people celebrating. All Emily could really make out from Matt was "Love you," and a Rocky Balboa-like "I can't talk long, I'm pretty tired."

Then he called Bernardino, his old coach.

"You're talking to an Ironman!" Matt said.

After the two phone calls, and another slice of pizza, Matt exited the recovery area, where he was able to give his parents an even tighter three-way hug. They kept taking pictures, smiling, and hugging him.

"Why don't you put something on," his mother told him.

"I'm not cold, Mom," he replied.

An e-mail came in from McIsaac: "Amazing time! Amazing accomplishment! Savor the moment."

Matt's father had told Michael and Linda to meet them after the race at the restaurant reserved by Endurance Sports Travel, but Matt wanted only to go back to the hotel and shower. He had done things in his triathlon suit that one can't speak about but that all triathletes understand and his top priority, his only priority, was a shower.

So they loaded his bike into a shuttle van, and the family piled in, and they drove 10 kilometers back to the hotel, and Matt was giddy and euphoric and high the whole way, talking about the race, and how he loved the crowds along the bike route and how he felt like he was in the Tour de France with all the screaming people and how he had followed the strategy on the bike to perfection keeping an even pace the entire way and how once he had finished the bike he knew he'd finish he race, and how he wasn't going to be doing any more Ironman triathlons, maybe not ever, but certainly not for a decade. Now he was going to focus on his medical school, and residency, and becoming a physician. But first he was going to shower, eat and sleep. And buy some post race Ironman apparel.

Matt spent Monday recovering in Cozumel. He had read about the risk of deep vein thrombosis, blood clots in the legs after extreme endurance events. Experts recommended competitors wait a day before getting on an airplane and Matt thought it wise. So he spent Monday around the pool, relaxing and recovering and studying. He'd brought his med school books. He honestly didn't feel that bad. On Tuesday, on his flight from Cozumel to Houston, he sat next to a paraplegic who had attempted his fifth ironman in Cozumel, and still hadn't been able to finish. This time, the man's recumbent bike had broken down well into the race. The man had done marathons before on his wheel-chair, and completed several half-Ironmans, and he was determined to finish a full Ironman. Matt was impressed by the man's determination and his independence, and Matt realized on that flight what he really had already known: that his own story paled in comparison with so many others, that the world was filled with remarkable people who were striving and overcoming, and that a wonderful part of life was giving your all in pursuit of a goal. Matt missed his connecting flight and Tuesday ended up being a marathon of its own. He didn't get into bed back in Philadelphia until after 2:00 a.m. Yet still, on a rainy, miserable Wednesday morning, he was seated in an auditorium by 8:00 a.m., just another medical student in just another anatomy lecture. And maybe that was the most beautiful, wonderful and extraordinary thing of all. For Matt Miller, life went on.

———

COURTESY OF TOM GRALISH/ THE PHILADELPHIA INQUIRER
MATT, A FIRST YEAR MEDICAL STUDENT, AT THE UNIVERSITY OF PENNSYLVANIA

A FAMILY PORTRAIT: MATT, EMILY, MIKE, NANCY, MICHAEL, LINDA.

PHOTO BY 2DIGITAL.
MATT RIDES IN THE IRONMAN WEARING HIS FULL-FACE HELMET

PHOTO BY 2DIGITAL.
MATT FINISHES THE IRONMAN AND CELEBRATES!

MATT AS BEST MAN WITH HIS BROTHER MICHAEL, THE GROOM.

Ken Gregory, the driver of the Porsche, still works three days a week repairing and rebuilding classic cars in Waynesboro. He still loves old cars and has a garage full of them – but not the Porsche he was driving on the day of the accident. He sold it in May 2011, nearly two and a half years later. He wasn't looking to sell it, but somebody coming over to consider another one of his cars liked it and bought it. Ken told the buyer the back story – how Matt nearly died – but the buyer wasn't dissuaded. Ken never did repair the dents or scrapes resulting from the accident with Matt, and couldn't really explain why. He had attempted other repairs and improvements over the following couple of years and they always turned out badly. "Everything I did to that car, it always fought me," he said. "A 15-minute project would turn into a day project." Ken said the new owner "loves the car and I hope he has a better mojo with it than I did." Ken did not believe selling the car would help him put the accident behind him for good. "That will never happen," he said, but added, "I don't have to look at it anymore. I won't be reminded as much, let's say that."

Until he agreed to an interview for this book, more than two years after the accident, Ken said he'd never spoken about it with anyone other than Mark and Mary Ann Harris. Not his mother or sisters, not his friends. Ken had heard about Matt's amazing recovery and accomplishments – medical school and the Ironman – and this had helped him in dealing with the accident. "It's great he's doing so well," Ken said. "That's all I could hope for." Ken also said that he had largely come to peace with the event, tucked it away in his past, and was getting along well in life. He was pleasant and laughed many times during the interview. "I'm fine," he said. "I don't like to think about it, but it doesn't really bother me."

Ken did grow emotional at times during our interview as he recounted that terrible day. "Really what kept me sane was that I knew I absolutely didn't do anything wrong," he said. "I was just at the wrong place at the wrong time. I wasn't speeding. I wasn't fiddling with my radio. It was just all of a sudden."

Ken Gregory said he didn't think it was a good idea to reach out to Matt or his family. He didn't think it would be beneficial to anyone, and he assumed the Millers must feel the same way. "I think it would be awkward," he said. "I don't really...I'd like to try to put it behind me. It's gradually happening. That would bring it all forward again."

He wished them the very best. But he very much wanted to leave the accident in the past and let time continue to work its healing magic for all.

Rudy Kahsar remained friendly with Matt after the accident. On occasion during their third year, and their fourth, Rudy would bring his trainer over to Matt's duplex on Montebello Circle and ride with him indoors, maybe watch a movie or a ballgame together as they did a two-hour ride. Rudy continued riding the Virginia countryside, and planned a big cycling trip with friends the summer after graduation, along the Pacific Coast from Southern California to Vancouver, B.C.

Early in that trip, Rudy said, one of his friends "crashed on a downhill on Big Sur. He hit a big rock and laid-out all over the road. He was bleeding everywhere. It was the same thing. I was in front, pulling."

When his friend crashed, Rudy immediately thought of Matt and his accident on the Blue Ridge Parkway, the worst day of Rudy's life. "It was like the first thing that flashed through my mind – Oh no, not again," Rudy said. He went with his friend to the hospital. Even though the injuries weren't nearly as serious, and they could have continued on their journey to Vancouver, Rudy suggested they just abort and fly home. The accident had scared Rudy as much as it scared his friend who fell.

When Matt went off to medical school, Rudy headed to Boulder to pursue a master's degree in chemical engineering at the University of Colorado. That area is a biking paradise, and Rudy got back on his bike, and still rides all the time. He still competes in triathlons. Rudy and Matt have kept in touch. "I think it's great that he is out training and racing, the bigger the better," Rudy said of Matt. "A lot of people asked me if I was going to quit triathlons after the accident," Rudy said, "but it's something I love doing, so I am still doing it. I think Matt is the same way. A quotation that I think I heard somewhere is that, `you can live your life in fear, or you can live your life.' That's sort of how I feel."

Chris Morrow did indeed sell his bike and stop riding – for a year. He had bad flashbacks after the accident, but they became less frequent over time. He was a year ahead of Matt and Rudy in school. After graduation, Chris moved to Washington, D.C., as planned, and worked for the economics consulting firm. After about a year, he bought a bike and started riding again. In fact, he started riding his bike to work, a commuter through the streets of Washington. After a couple months, he stopped. He decided this wasn't such a great idea. But he continued riding occasionally, for exercise, in what he called "more controlled circumstances." "It's not necessarily something I need to be afraid of for the rest of my life," Chris said of cycling. "It's just something I need to approach more seriously."

Chris has also decided to change careers, to apply to medical school, to become a doctor. He said Matt's accident had much to do with his decision. "That is a moment I've come back to a lot, as I'm thinking about where it is I want to take my life," Chris said. He said he thinks not so much about the collision, but the moments after – "how Dr. Harris was able to respond with an incredible coolness. And the miracle of how he seemed to be there."

Chris has come to realize that he wants to take a more direct role in people's lives. He wants to have more impact, more contact, than sitting behind a desk analyzing data. And reflecting on the day of Matt's accident has helped him see his own life and future path more clearly.

Mark Harris retired from his medical practice in the summer of 2011, after 33 years as an anesthesiologist. He hoped to travel with his wife and enjoy his classic cars. Mark and Mary Ann Harris consider the Millers friends for life, and Mary Ann said of Matt, "He's one of ours now."

Bruce Singer, the dentist who restored Matt's beautiful smile, died in January of 2012 from complications after surgery. It was a shocking, tragic loss.

All of the Millers realize every day how much they've been blessed and the blessings keep coming. Michael and Linda were married in August, 2011, in the University of Virginia chapel. Matt was the best man.

Matt has continued his remarkable recovery. His facial nerves have nearly fully healed with the passage of time, and his facial function is largely restored. He will never look as he did before the accident, but nobody meeting him for the first time, or passing him on the street, would ever suspect the trauma he had endured. There is little visible evidence of it.

Both Matt and Emily did well in their first two years of medical school, and have begun clinical rotations to figure out their areas of specialty. No decisions yet. Matt continues to feel healthy, to bike, run or swim daily, and to compete in road races and smaller triathlons. And contrary to what he said in Mexico, he's thinking already about another Ironman – possibly when he's in his fourth year of medical school. When Matt visits Dr. Meltzer every two months for cleanings and maintenance of his teeth, the office staff greets him with a chorus of, "Matt Miller, Ironman!"

And one other piece of news: Matt got down on one knee in December of 2011 and proposed to Emily before dinner at one of Philadelphia's most romantic restaurants. They plan to marry right before graduating from medical school in the spring of 2014.

• • •

And that is exactly what happened!

And the story gets even better.

Matt and Emily will return in June of 2014 to Charlottesville, and Matt will become a resident physician at the University of Virginia Hospital working with Doctors Park and Christophel – the same facial trauma surgeons who rebuilt his face after the accident and saved his life.

Matt said he knew early on in medical school he wanted to be a surgeon, and soon it became clear to him that he wanted to do for others what these skilled surgeons had done for him. That Virginia worked out as the best place for him and Emily now seems inevitable. It is worth remembering here that Matt wrote his senior honors thesis about the history of this very department of otolaryngology. Even Matt had to laugh when reminded of this fact.

"It's very special to be able to work with the people who saved my life," Matt said.

"It really felt like fate," added Emily, who will do her residency in dermatology also at UVa.

"We are thrilled to have him," said Park. "I have no doubt he would have excelled anywhere." It was Park who noted back at the time of the accident, as he observed Matt's incredible recovery up close, that it was not his empathy for patients that one day would make him a great surgeon, but his relentless pursuit of perfection.

"We were thrilled to hear that Matt matched with us," said Christophel, at the time of the accident Park's chief resident but now a surgeon in the department. "Matt is an absolutely stellar candidate and could have gone anywhere in the country. We are humbled that he chose to come here and very much looking forward to having him as one of our residents. If he continues to work as hard as he has, he'll be one of the leaders in our field."

Matt and Emily were married at the Chapel of Four Chaplains in the Philadelphia Navy Yard. Mark Harris, the anesthesiologist who saved Matt's life on the mountain, sat in one of the front rows with his wife, Mary Ann. Mark Bernardino, Matt's former swim coach at Virginia who became a coach for him in the hospital, motivating him every day, read a poem by Emerson in the service.

Bride and groom each wrote vows. Matt recounted how Emily held his hand through the night, every night, as he was recovering in the hospital.

"You always have done everything possible to make sure I am the happiest person in the world," he told her. He also told her at the altar: "You are the only person who I can tell anything to you, who I can truly be myself around. I never have to try to impress you. You know how silly I can be, how ridiculous I can get, yet you still love me for exactly who I am."

He promised to always be there to love her, listen to her, support her and make the coffee in the morning because, "I know that even though I have told you many times how to make it, you still have trouble."

In her vows, she recounted how when they started dating, he sent her song lyrics, and when they attended different colleges for the first two years (she went to East Carolina), he sent a new lyric without fail every day.

"I love that you are always thinking of me and are so dedicated to our relationship," she told him. "There is no one I would rather talk to about my day, laugh with, or ask for reassurance and guidance. You are so open, and I always feel that we understand each other so completely."

She ended her vows by citing a favorite lyric from the band U2 that he once sent:

"A blue-eyed boy meets a brown-eyed girl, oh oh oh, the sweetest thing."

• • •

Like on Facebook: The Road Back: A Journey of Grace and Grit
Get updates and follow the author on Twitter @michaelvitez
Read more of his stories, follow his blog: Readmichaelvitez.tumblr.com

Photograph © Lauren Fair Photography

ACKNOWLEDGEMENTS

This journey for me started at a poker game. I work for The Philadelphia Inquirer, and have for 27 years. All I've ever known is newspapering. A group of reporters at the Inquirer – maybe 20 years ago now – started a poker game every third Sunday. It is a friendly game, for modest stakes, and one might win or lose around $25 after an evening of poker. I often lose but love it nonetheless.

Many in the group have left the newspaper business but stayed in the poker game. One, Craig Stock, a good friend and former columnist and business editor at the Inquirer, went to work in the mid-90s at Vanguard. At poker one night, sitting on Paul Nussbaum's back deck, after Paul had grilled some chicken for the group and we were about to get started, Craig told me a story. Craig knew I had gone to UVA back in the day, and he shared with me the story of his boss, Mike Miller, and Mike's son, Matt. I told Craig this was not only a great story, but a great story for the newspaper. I approached the Millers and what resulted was a three-part series that ran in the Inquirer. That received such an incredible reaction – and Matt continued to make such an amazing recovery – that I decided to write this book.

I owe a great debt to Craig not only for giving me the idea, but for reading the book and making suggestions and being so supportive all along.

I also owe a great debt to all the people in the book who trusted me, who let me into their lives, who were so giving of their time. I especially want to thank all the doctors who were patient with me, helping me understand the medicine involved. I also want to offer special thanks to the emergency responders, who gave me a window into their intense world.

I honestly can't begin to thank the Miller family, and Emily, for their faith and support and assistance. I asked so much of them. I want to thank Ken Gregory for revisiting an extremely painful moment in his life, and for trusting me. That also goes for Rudy Kahsar and Chris Morrow, both of whom have exceptionally bright futures.

I am grateful to Peter Landry, a great friend and former colleague, for reading this book and making invaluable suggestions. I also must thank my friend and fellow 'Hoo, Jim Rowe, for his thoughts and comments. Even though we couldn't hook the big New York publishers, Christy Fletcher and Alyssa Wolff at Fletcher and Company never quit on me and I am grateful.

Thanks to Rachel Caldwell for her fabulous cover design.

Most of all I want to thank my family, in particular my wife, Maureen. It is difficult to live with someone who is going through such an emotional and trying process as writing and selling a book. She was endlessly patient and supportive, and on top of all that provided me with great editing and brilliant suggestions – like the title.

I see this book as a story that shows America at its very best. Family, community, professionals and institutions all shine here. It is not a perfect story. There is tragedy and heartbreak along the way as well as triumph. But isn't that life?

ABOUT THE AUTHOR

 Michael T. Vitez has been a staff writer at The Philadelphia Inquirer for 27 years. He won the 1997 Pulitzer Prize for explanatory journalism. Vitez has taught classes in narrative non-fiction at the University of Pennsylvania and was a visiting Ferris Professor of Journalism at Princeton. He is also a former Michigan Journalism Fellow. He is the author of *Rocky Stories: Tales of Love, Hope and Happiness at America's Most Famous Steps.* (2006) He graduated from the University of Virginia, where he was editor-in-chief of The Cavalier Daily. He is married to Maureen Fitzgerald, food editor at the Inquirer, and they have three children. And for 12 years, he has organized an annual triathlon at his local swim club!

Made in the USA
Charleston, SC
29 July 2014